THE WAY THAT WATER ENTERS STONE

Stories

John Dufresne

W · W · Norton & Company
New York · London

Printed in the United States of America.

The text of this book is composed in Linotype
Walbaum,
with the display set in Futura Light.
Composition and manufacturing by the Maple-
Vail Book Manufacturing Group.
Book design by Guenet Abraham.

Lyrics from the following song have been used:
"That's the Way Love Is" by Norman Whitfield/
Barrett Strong. © 1966 Stone Agate Music.

First Edition

Library of Congress Cataloging-in-Publication
Data

Dufresne, John.
The way that water enters stone : stories /
John Dufresne.
p.   cm.
I. Title
PS3554.U325W39   1991
813'.54—dc20   90–38997

ISBN 0–393–02924–7

W.W. Norton & Company, Inc.
500 Fifth Avenue, New York, N.Y. 10110
W.W. Norton & Company, Ltd.
10 Coptic Street, London, WC1A 1PU

1 2 3 4 5 6 7 8 9 0

For my parents, Doris and Lefty,
and for Cindy and Tristan

So you take it where you find it,
Or leave it like it is.
That's the way it's always been,
That's the way love is.

— Bobby Blue Bland,
"That's the Way Love Is"

CONTENTS

ACKNOWLEDGMENTS

The author gratefully acknowledges the following magazines in which these stories first appeared in somewhat different form:

Missouri Review: "People That Dream, Whales That Dance"
The Quarterly: "The Freezer Jesus," "What Follows in the Wake of Love"
Yankee: "To Save a Life," "The Slow Death of the B Movie" (previously titled "The Promise of the Rialto"), "A Long Line of Dreamers"
"Surveyors" was a selection in the 1984 PEN Syndicated Fiction Awards and appeared in several newspapers and *The Available Press / PEN Short Story Collection* (Ballatine Books, 1985) and in *Lives in Translation: An Anthology of Contemporary Franco-American Writings* (Soleil Press, 1990).

Further appreciation is due the *Translantic Review* / Henfield Foundation, whose financial assistance provided time to work on these stories.

And thanks to William Harrison and James Whitehead.

THE · WAY · THAT · WATER
ENTERS·STONE

PROVIDENCE

MISS LANGEVIN COULD write a book on disappoint-
ment. She'd tell the reader you can't depend on people,
not really, not when it counts. Mention how she met this
sailor home from the war, just off his ship, at the Kittery
Naval Base. He told her he'd dreamed of this day every
night for two and a half years, took her to New York City
for the victory parades. She wore his white cap; they talked
themselves breathless about this future that opened before
them like a spring flower. None of the others would be
quite so handsome as that Charles O'Leary, so full of grat-
itude and hope.

Since her father died eighteen years ago, Miss Lan-
gevin has lived alone in their house off Route 22 near
Gorham, the same tidy four rooms she was raised in. It
would be simple to succumb to loneliness there, but point-
less. Miss Langevin will not rely on solitude. One should
be with people, naturally, she would write, but one should
expect nothing.

Each May 15, Miss Langevin locks her cottage and
returns to the Burgoyne House in Old Orchard Beach,
where for three and a half months she manages the guest
house for Mrs. Berard; lives among strangers, Canadians
mostly; launders linen; registers guests; purchases sup-
plies; and deposits money in Mrs. Berard's account at the
Biddeford Savings Bank up on Saco Avenue. She works
with whomever Mrs. Berard hires as cleaning lady that
season, usually a college girl from Orono. The house con-
sists of two floors, three triple rooms, six doubles, with cots
available for two dollars a night.

Mrs. Berard, wearing her son's red hunting jacket and
green woolen mittens, rocks in an armless wicker chair on
the tiny front porch of the Burgoyne. Across the street,
behind Desjardin's Superette, an aproned clerk stacks
plastic milk crates. Mrs. Berard remembers when Old
Orchard was quite the resort—the grand hotels, the trains
up from Boston, down from Portland, parasoled ladies and
boatered gentlemen promenading on the pier. Once, with
her mother, she saw John Barrymore himself, drink in hand,
standing on the veranda of the old Olympia Hotel, staring
off into Saco Bay. Now the rich stay in Ogunquit or Ken-

nebunkport. There are no more passenger trains. Mrs.
Berard stops, listens to the ringing telephone in the foyer.
Sure, she could sell the Burgoyne, but then what?
"Mrs. Berard."
"Yes, Miss Langevin?"
"The new cleaning girl. She's on her way."
"I'll be in directly."
She remembers the long and dazzling summers of her
youth, the walks with Alain along the beach to Pine Point,
driving the skiff to Prouts Neck for picnics, watching for
blue herons on the Scarborough Marsh. Once, after Roger
was born, Alain sat with her in the gazebo, right there
where the driveway is now, and said, "You know, Agnes,
we're really good for each other." Every year carries her
further from Alain, and every May her sadness blooms
like the crocuses.

Doris, the new cleaning woman, arrives at six every
morning, an hour early, and quietly as she can, she perks
a pot of coffee before even starting in with the mop. Miss
Langevin had that same kind of energy when she started
at the Burgoyne eighteen years ago. She was only forty-
one then and was still trying to impress herself with her
ambition and potential. Miss Langevin figures Doris is even
younger than that, maybe thirty-fivish. Actually, Doris is
twenty-nine and lives in town with her husband, who's out
of work again. She'd like to be able to save money for
once. To say to her husband, we can leave this town, we
can start a family now. She works like she's afraid if she
stops, she'll collapse. Miss Langevin admires Doris's zeal,

even wishes she could be so single-minded, but believes it is all so insignificant, now that she's beyond her promise.

On Memorial Day, Mrs. Berard packs her two leather suitcases and summons Doris and Miss Langevin to the kitchen for final instructions. Have oil delivered on the 15th. Call the yard man before that catalpa limb falls on the porch roof. Mr. Potvin will be along to repair the window sash in number 4. Ask him to check that loose baluster on the second floor. She tells them goodbye.

Mrs. Berard will visit her cousins in Montreal until the Fourth of July. This morning is the first time the three women have sat together to talk. Mrs. Berard opens a bobby pin with her front teeth, then reaches to fasten a lock of hair behind her ear. "Doris, dear," she says, "Miss Langevin tells me you're a wonderful worker, the best we've had."

Doris thanks them both, blushes. There is quiet. In seventh grade, her project on mycoplasmas won the junior high science fair and so many people talked at her, embarrassed her with congratulations, that she couldn't think, wound up crying and running out of the church hall. She would never make a show of herself again.

"It's just you and your husband then, Doris?" Mrs. Berard asks. "No little ones?"

"Just the two of us."

"That's right, you're young yet. Enjoy each other."

Before she catches the bus to Portland Airport, Mrs. Berard will stop at the cemetery in Saco to lay wreaths at the graves of her husband and only child. She'll pluck the taller blades of grass that grow against the headstones, say three Our Fathers, three Hail Marys, three Glory Bes. By then, Doris will have turned the beds in the first-floor rooms, Miss Langevin have spoken to the young couple in number 7 to see if they'll be staying another night.

Miss Langevin is in her room at the end of the first-floor corridor behind the French doors. She has the black-and-white TV tuned to a soap opera. There's a band of tinfoil wrapped around the antenna, but the reception remains ghostly. She's ironing linen, staring out at the chilly rain as it tattoos the fiberglass roof over the entryway to the American Legion Hall. She's thinking of the turns her life has taken, imagining what she might be doing just now, in some other place or places. Doris has set her off. On Monday, Doris arrived to work in tears that she blamed on allergies. Her upper lip was swollen and her left cheek bruised beneath the eye.

Miss Langevin considers that she could still be teaching second grade in Sanford, which she did till she was nearly forty. Gave up twelve years in the system, and for what? Or she might have been in California right now like Mr. Wallace Plunkett, then principal of Sanford Elementary, promised. But why dig that up again?

"Miss Langevin."

"Come in, Doris."

Doris closes the door, holds the knob behind her in both hands. Miss Langevin lifts a pile of folded linen from the Morris chair.

Doris touches the arm of the chair. "I won't be staying,"

she says. She forces a smile, takes a long breath, and looks at the floor. "I just . . . well, I don't want you to worry about . . . you know."

"Yes."

"It's just that it's hard right now with Richie. We'll do okay. Really."

"Of course you will."

Through all of July and August, Old Orchard's population swells fifteen times to a hundred thousand or more. Days are brilliant, warm. Herons wade among the long grasses in the salt marsh. Families crowd their way past the food stalls and arcades to the beach and seven miles of white sand. At night, the recurrent rev of motorcycle engines roars above the blare of the amusement park. From her bedroom, Doris can see the pier, an isthmus of light, and can hear the calypso band that plays the nightclub there. Some nights she listens until the music fades, and the shrieks from the bar stop. Then she hears the surf, the wind through a plane tree, the footfall of a solitary walker, flip-flops slapping at his heels as he passes beneath her window. Then she sleeps.

Doris sits at the counter in Marie's Café, sips coffee, and imagines it's September already and the maples are turning. The sky is low, leaden, the streets deserted. Restaurants close early at first, then for the season. Amusement rides are disassembled until only their bony frames rest in the fog. Shops are boarded up. Once again Doris is slapped with the knowledge that she'll be left behind. She shivers. Not this year.

If only she could convince Richie to leave. How? They can't move without money, and they can't save money. That's what the fight was about. She knew he wanted something when he was so cuddly after supper. Sweetheart, I need twenty for the track, he said when they finished making love. She told him there wasn't much, and it was savings, and anyway, it was hers. That was when he punched her, once.

"You okay, honey?"

Doris wipes her eyes with a napkin. "Hay fever, Marie, that's all."

"Here's more coffee." Marie fills her cup. "You sure?"

"Sure."

It's reached the point that she's glad he doesn't come home every night. Then she can sleep at least. If only she had children, she thinks. Richie won't talk about that. And really, what chance would a child of theirs have? Doris slides two quarters under the lip of her saucer, sops up her place with the napkin, puts the napkin in the cup. She slips out the door.

Last night, long after the pier had vanished in the darkness, long after Richie had slammed the screen door and scattered driveway gravel with his Harley, in her dream a man stepped off a train from Montreal. He was smartly dressed, had one blue eye, one brown eye. He walked up to Doris in front of Desjardin's and asked if she knew of a vacant room. That's when the four-twenty freight from Augusta rattled her awake as it whistled through the Atlantic Avenue crossing.

Doris smiles at her reflection in the souvenir-shop window, bares her teeth, slides her tongue across the uppers, blots her lips, examines her profile. A man could walk right up to her, speak with her, be taken by her quiet charms. She'll do something with the hair. And he might be handsome, single, and tender.

Mrs. Berard's first postcard arrives. It's a photo of the shrine of Ste. Anne de Beaupré. She writes that her cousins are worried about her shortness of breath and fainting spells. She'll be glad to return to the salt air. Miss Langevin tacks the card to the doorjamb in the kitchen. She notices Doris walking through Desjardin's parking lot on her way back from lunch. Doris spots her, waves. Doris smiles, sees herself in a city, the morning sun slants through the kitchen window, she sips coffee, listens to the singing from the shower.

"Good afternoon, Miss Langevin."

"You seem in a better mood."

"I'm sorry about this morning."

"Don't be silly."

Doris sits at the kitchen table while Miss Langevin takes a phone call in the office. She reminds herself there are no Prince Charmings. No man will step off a train to sweep her away. If she wants a different life, she'll have to leave Richie.

Miss Langevin returns. "We'll need a cot in number eight for Friday."

"Miss Langevin, have you ever been to Providence?"

"Providence? No. Went to New York once. The rest of the time I've been right around here."

"I've never lived anywhere but this town. Great place to be a little kid, but . . . I've got a cousin Charlene in Providence. I think I may visit. It might do me some good."

"Yes. Sometimes a holiday will clear the air."

The rain has stopped. Miss Langevin walks to the pier. Benches are wet, beach empty. She wonders, without knowing why, if Doris might have seen her and her lover, Mr. Plunkett, when they took their one weekend at the beach in 1967. Perhaps Doris was one of the adorable, tiny pigtailed girls building sand castles that she pointed out to Wallace. They stayed at the Burgoyne and giggled about the old lady who ran the place, who was so concerned that they be legally married. "If you don't want our business, Mrs. Berard, Mrs. Plunkett and I will call on another establishment." Miss Langevin had tried not to laugh.

She remembers every detail. That Sunday after Mass, he took her to the Marie Antoinette Restaurant. They waited in line by the cash register behind a man holding a *Globe*, wearing wing-tips and no socks. His pink arms were peeling. Wallace took a toothpick from the shot glass beside the register. They sat across from each other at a table for four by the window. The menu was printed in French and English on the plastic placemats. They ate toast, ordered coffee.

"But I never asked you to leave your wife, Wallace."

Coffee arrived. Wallace asked the waitress for more cream. Miss Langevin said, "I can't believe this."

"Don't you see I'm trying to do the right thing for all of us here?"

"I'm not convenient anymore?"

"What's that supposed to mean?"

"Just that you're so predictable."

Wallace thanked the waitress, lightened his coffee, took a sip, and wiped his mustache with the edge of a napkin.

"The weekend," she said, "the restaurant, the trite but obligatory farewell scene with the other woman."

"You think I'm enjoying this?"

"Tell me what to do, Wallace."

"I can't do that."

"Then tell me why it hurts so much."

"You think I'm not hurt?"

"Oh, Jesus, Wallace."

"Why am I the bad guy? Tell me that. You knew what you were doing."

"Thank you for that, Wallace."

'Look, I'm sorry. I . . ."

"No, you're right. I got what I deserved. Ask anybody." Miss Langevin found a Kleenex in her purse. She blew her nose. "All better," she said. She smiled. Wallace motioned for the check. The man with the pink arms stared at them from his table across the dining room. She caught his eyes.

"Shall we go?" Wallace said.

"Will you tell her?"

"My wife?"

"About the last three years."

"It would kill her."
"Shall I?"

Doris wonders why she told Miss Langevin about Prov-
idence. She shakes her head, orders a drink. She carries
the drink to a cushioned bench by the picture window.
Doris crosses her legs, adjusts the purse on her lap, looks
out to where the gray neck of land dissolves into the white
sky. She has no cousin in Providence. Charlene was her
mother's name. Maybe she wanted to reassure Miss Lan-
gevin, announce that she need accept no responsibility for
any of it, not the bruised eye and not the future. I can get
free of this place is what she was telling Miss Langevin.
    Instead of walking straight home from work, Doris has
stopped at the patio bar on the pier. She senses that this is
a desperate act. She's never done anything this unex-
pected. Never left her house without leaving a note for
Richie. Doris stares at her highball glass, takes a breath
and smiles. So what *would* she do? Where *would* she go?
Not some other resort. Doris stirs her drink. Some shelter-
ing town. She thinks, Ohio, and pictures tight, snug houses,
fields of grain, a gothic town hall, cloth coats and polite
nods. She hears Richie's voice.
    His back is to her. He's leaning on his elbow at the bar
and he's laughing with the bartender and a woman. His
mirror sunglasses are pushed up on his head. Doris sees
the rolls at his hips beneath the black T-shirt. The wom-
an's left hand clutches his right elbow. Jesus, Doris whis-
pers. She has to leave before he turns around and sees her.
The woman's hands are now clasped around Richie's sun-

burned neck. Richie orders a round for the house. The woman's hair is red and curled. The bartender rings a ship's bell over the bar, which elicits cheers from the patrons, who begin a rhythmical applause. The woman slides her hands into Richie's back pockets and pulls him close. His arms are straight out. He pretends to fly. They kiss, the drinkers whoop, call for more.

Doris slips out the door.

Richie comes home sometime after four-twenty and collapses, boots and all, on their bed. Doris tosses. She smells the woman on his shirt. If she could sleep, she could dream. She listens to her husband snore.

Doris closes her eyes and tries to picture the man at the train or a man in a hardware store in Ohio. She looks at Richie. Once when he was trim he took her to Ogunquit to walk along the rocks.

It's dawn. She gets up, coaxes some help from her sleeping husband, removes his boots, jeans, and shirt. She covers him with a sheet and a cotton blanket. In the kitchen, Doris drinks her first cup of coffee and does a load of wash.

This is the phone call Miss Langevin has been expecting. She doesn't know how she knows, but she knows. In her second postcard, Mrs. Berard wrote that she wouldn't be home for the Fourth after all. The Canadian weather has played havoc with her constitution.

"Miss Langevin?"

"Yes."

"Miss Langevin, this is Ora Falling, Agnes Berard's cousin."

"She's dead."

"Yes."

"I'm sorry."

At the grave, days after the funeral, Miss Langevin speaks with Doris. She tells her the family has decided to sell the Burgoyne at season's end. Not to worry, the two of them will be paid through Labor Day. Miss Langevin and Doris have come to plant the bulbs that will bloom next spring.

Doris stares at the grave. "Did you know her well, Miss Langevin?"

"As well as anyone did, I suppose. Her husband and son died in a wreck on the turnpike thirty years ago. She had the Burgoyne, never liked the summer crowds, but couldn't bear to leave for good. Sundays she sang in the choir at St. Luke's."

"I remember her, you know. When we were kids, my brother and I played handball against Desjardin's back wall. We would see her rocking on the porch. Timmy thought she was spooky."

"Imagine."

"Strange how things turn out."

"You end up working for her. You couldn't have expected that."

"I never figured I'd have to work at all. I'd marry some handsome boy, a realtor maybe, and he'd give me a home, children, spending money. I had it all worked out. Didn't you?"

"Maybe not a realtor."

"I was sure I'd be taken care of."

"Yes." There is quiet. Miss Langevin smoothes the earth with her trowel. Still kneeling, she prays silently. Doris bows her head.

"Amen."

They walk the gravelly path to the gates. Miss Langevin looks at Doris, turns her eyes to the road ahead, says, "Do you find it at all disappointing, Doris?"

"What disappointing?"

"Forgive me. Just thinking out loud."

The red-haired woman works at the Beachcomber. Doris finds her tending bar on Saturday morning. Richie's home asleep. She tells the woman she looks familiar. Have they met somewhere or something?

"Maybe you've seen me at one of the clubs," she says. She puts down her cigarette and waits on a customer. She pours him a draft. She returns. "Freshen that up for you?"

"Not yet."

"My boyfriend and I step out a lot. He likes to dance."

"That's it," Doris says. "Don't you go out with Richie St. Germaine?"

"You know Richie?" The woman lifts Doris's glass and wipes the bar with a damp rag. "He ain't much, I know, but what are your choices around here, know what I mean?"

"I do."

"So you must be from town."

"I thought he was married."

The woman tosses the bar rag at the steel sink. "Yeah," she says, "he's not even close to perfect."

Doris is puzzled by her own serenity.

"Ready for another?"

With Doris gone, Miss Langevin has the final few hours of the Burgoyne to herself. Her bags are packed and sitting on the front porch. She stuffs the rosary beads, the Bible, and the snapshot of her and her father on the carousel into her purse. She's forgotten who took the picture. Maybe her mother. She goes upstairs, opens doors, walks into Room 6 for the last time. She knows she can't come back. She wishes Doris were here.

Doris stopped by early this morning on her way to the bus station. "We've hardly gotten to know each other," she said. They hugged. Doris kissed Miss Langevin on the cheek. "Take care of yourself," she said. And then she left. Doris did the right thing. She'll like Providence.

The American Legion has bought the building. By next spring, the site will be leveled and paved. In the kitchen, Miss Langevin studies Mrs. Berard's postcard. People on their knees are climbing the long steps of the shrine. There's a knock at the door.

"Good morning."

"I'm sorry, sir, we're closed."

"Miss Langevin?"

"Yes."

The tall young man takes off his ball cap, clears his throat, smiles. "Excuse me." He looks beyond Miss Langevin's shoulder.

"Can I help you?"

"May I come in? This is personal."

Miss Langevin leads the young man to the office. They sit. "Are you a relative of Mrs. Berard?"

"No, ma'am." He leans forward in his chair, rubs his knee with his hand. "My name is Richie St. Germaine."

Miss Langevin watches Richie. He's looking around at the furniture.

He says, "Doris's husband."

"Yes."

Miss Langevin tells him she doesn't know where Doris is. He confesses he hasn't been the best husband. He just wants to call her, is all, ask her for one more chance. Miss Langevin thinks about men, how they try to be sweet when they need to be. He tells her a wife's place is with her husband.

"Unless there's a reason not to be."

"My, my, Miss Langevin." Richie stands. He puts his cap on, laughs.

"Perhaps you should leave, sir."

"As soon as you tell me where she is."

"I don't know."

"You're lying."

"I don't know who you think you're dealing with, young man."

"A senile old bitch."

"Get out!"

Richie approaches Miss Langevin. She can smell motor oil on his down vest. She won't move. He stands over her and burps. He whispers her Gorham address into her ear. She pulls her head away from his. Got it off the luggage tags. He grabs her chin, pinches her face in his hand. "I'll burn your house with you in it," he says, puts his nose to hers, squeezes her jaw. "I'll just bet your bones are hollow like a bird's."

"Please." She is crying.

"Don't think I won't do it."

"Providence."

"What?"

"She went to Providence."

"That's more like it." He releases her face, backs her to the wall. "You wouldn't be lying to Richie, would you?" He places the heel of his boot on her left foot. "Where in Providence?" She hesitates. He raises his boot, smiles.

"All right, I'll tell you." She wipes her nose. He doesn't know any cousin Charlene, but never mind, he says, he'll find her. No city big enough to hide from him.

"Damn right. I'll find her and drag her back where she belongs. Thanks to you, dear."

"You won't find her."

"Oh, you better hope I do, or I'll be paying you another visit. With my gasoline can."

Miss Langevin shuts her eyes. Richie lifts a Burgoyne business card from the corner of the blotter on the desktop. "Something to remember you by," he says.

Miss Langevin slumps to the floor, back against the wall. Her head aches. She's going to be sick. Richie hunkers in front of her. He thanks her, takes her hand and crushes it, hears a crack. She moans.

"I told you so," he says.

When Miss Langevin wakes, she is on her bed in the

dark behind the French doors. Her hand throbs. He'll never find Doris, she thinks. She sits up, settles the dizziness, then shifts her legs over the side of the bed.

The Burgoyne is closed, the power is off, phone disconnected. She has to leave. She stands. She imagines Doris asleep on a bus. Miss Langevin thinks of her own inland cottage, of the long season ahead. She examines her swollen hand. Something is broken.

THE FREEZER JESUS

TWO DAYS AFTER we learned we had Jesus on our freezer, my sister Elvie had this dream where all the mystery was explained to her. Freezer's this ordinary, yellow Amana. Sets out there on the porch on account of we got no room for it inside the house. What Jesus explained to Elvie in the dream was that He supernaturally connected the porch light to the freezer and turned the freezer into a TV and on that TV was Jesus Himself. Elvie, He says to her, I've chosen you and your brother Arlis this time because you all been so alone and so good these fifty, sixty years and because your bean crop's going to fail again this spring.

And tell Arlis, He said, to call the Monroe newspaper and tell them Jesus has come again and everyone should know what that means.

Now, I've never been a strictly religious person like most of my neighbors. Naturally, I believe in the Lord and salvation and Satan and all of that. I just never reckoned what all that had to do with planting beans or chopping cotton, you see. And then comes that Friday and I'm walking Elvie up the path from the bean field at dusk and I notice the porch light on and I tell Elvie we must have had a visitor stop by. As we get closer, I notice a blemish on the freezer door that wasn't there before. Then suddenly the blemish erupts like a volcano and commences to changing shape, and what were clouds at first become a beard and hair, and I recognize immediately and for certain that the image is the very face of Jesus right down to the mole near his left eye.

What is it, Arlis? Elvie says to me. Why you shaking? Of course Elvie can't see what I see because she's blind as a snout beetle. So I tell her about this Jesus, and somehow she knows it's true and falls to her knees and sobs. Praise God, Arlis, she says.

We're not accustomed to much excitement in Holly Ridge, Louisiana. Only time we made the news was seven years ago when a twelve-point buck jumped through Leamon Dozier's bathroom window while he was shaving and thrashed itself to unconsciousness. Still, the Dream Jesus had told Elvie we were to let the world know, so I called the paper. The boy they sent along didn't mind telling me

he was mighty skeptical before he witnessed the freezer
with his own eyes. Said, though, it looked more like Willie
Nelson than Jesus unless you squinted your eyes, and then
it looked like the Ayatollah of Iran. Of course, any way
you look at it, he said, it's a miracle. He took out his little
notebook and asked Elvie what she thought this means.
She said, well, this here's Jesus, and evidently He has cho-
sen Richland Parish for His Second Coming. My advice,
she told the boy, is that people should get ready.

First off, just a few people came at twilight to watch the
freezer erupt with Jesus. Then they brought friends. Then
the gospel radio station in Rayville hired a bus and drove
folks out here. Pretty soon, the Faulkner Road was crowded
all the way to 138 with dusty pilgrims. I spent my after-
noons and evenings trying to regulate the toilet line through
the house. Either that or I'd be fetching water from the
well for the thirsty or faint or trying to keep the cars off
my melon patch. Anyway, I got little work done in the
fields and soon the Johnson grass had choked the life from
my beans. Elvie reminded me how the Lord had prophe-
sied the crop failure, and she reassured me that He would
provide.

Every night at nine-thirty, the Amana TV would begin
to fade slowly and within minutes the divine image would
be gone. Then I'd spend an hour or so picking up soda
cans and candy wrappers all over the yard. Once in a while
I'd find a pilgrim still lingering by the coop, up to some-
thing, I don't know what, and I'd have to ask him to leave.
One time this Italian lady from Vicksburg says to me could

she have a morsel of food that I kept in the freezer. She
was sure if she could just eat something out of that holy
freezer, she would be cured of her stomach cancer. I gave
her a channel cat I'd caught in Bayou Macon and said I
hoped it worked.

Then this TV evangelist drove up from Baton Rouge in
a long, white limousine, walked up on the porch, looked
the freezer up and down without a word, followed the arc
of the extension cord plugged into the porch light, gazed
out at the gape-mouthed crowd, turned to me, smiled sort
of, said Praise Jesus in a whispery voice, combed his fin-
gers through his long hair, nodded to his chauffeur, got
back into the limousine, and drove away.

The TV minister wasn't the only preacher who came
calling. The Reverend Danny Wink from the True Vine
Powerhouse Pentecostal Church came every day and took
to sitting beside Elvie in a seat of honor, I suppose he
thought, up on the porch by the screen door. It was the
Reverend Wink's idea to transfer the freezer to his church,
where it could be worshiped properly before a splendid
congregation and all, which was sure okay with me so long
as the Reverend furnished us with another freezer. I had
a shelf full of crawfish tails to think about. Elvie, though,
told him she was waiting on a sign from Jesus. One eve-
ning, the Reverend Wink presented Elvie with a brass
plaque that read: "This Freezer Donated by Elvie and Arlis
Elrod," and pointed to where he'd screw it onto the freezer.

About a month after Jesus first appeared to us, I'm
sleeping when I hear this racket out on the porch and I get

up quietly, figuring it's one of the idolaters come back in the middle of the night to fool with the freezer. What I see, though, is Elvie kneeling in a pool of light from the open freezer door, holding handfuls of ice cubes over her eyelids, weeping, asking Jesus to scrub the cataracts from her milky old eyes. I watched Elvie for three nights running. On that last night, Elvie started jabbering in tongues the way the Reverend Wink does, and she's so like a lunatic there in her nightgown screaming at this big, cold machine that I can't watch no more.

In the morning, I found Elvie slumped on the kitchen floor. She said, Arlis, I'm as blind as dirt and always will be. She called the Reverend Wink and had him haul off the freezer that morning. And then what happened was this:

Jesus never did reappear on that freezer, which made the believers at the True Vine Powerhouse Church angry and vengeful. Right from his pulpit, the Reverend Wink called me and Elvie schemers, charlatans, and tools of the Devil. Elvie, herself, grew bitter and remote, asked me did I do something clever with that Amana maybe. I said no I didn't, and she said it surely wasn't kind of the Lord to give her hope and then snatch it away like He done. Our bean crop's ruined, cotton's all leggy and feeble, and I don't know what we'll do.

Can't even say the Lord will provide, but I do know that He's still here with us. I see Him everywhere I look, only this time I'm keeping the news to myself. I saw Him in that cloud that dropped a lightning bolt this afternoon. I see His face in the knot on the trunk of that live oak out back. What I notice this time is those peculiar wine-dark eyes, drunk with the sadness of rutted fields and empty rooms. I can squint my eyes and see Jesus smiling back at me from the dots on the linoleum floor, and I think He must be comforted by my attention. I hear His voice in the wind calling to me, and I feel calm. I hear Him whisper, Arlis, get ready. In her room, Elvie sits at the edge of the bed, coughs once in a while, and fingers the hem of her housedress.

A LONG LINE
OF DREAMERS

THE LEOMINSTER HIGH Blue Devil Marching Band wants eleven replacement trombones and three snare drums and wants them by Friday afternoon. I should hop to it and fill this order. I should but I can't. It's this business with Cliff. It's making me sad or sick or something. I figure if I write it all out like I'm doing here, maybe I'll feel better.

That used to work for me in high school. I wrote poems when I was sad. I would sit in my room for hours with a dictionary trying to uncover rhymes for "snob" and "McDermott." And I always did feel better afterwards, not

that I was any good at poetry really. Geography was my
subject. I loved to stare at the shapes and the colors of the
countries on the wall maps and listen to Mr. Tripodi pro-
nounce those faraway names like Ulan Bator and Nyasa-
land. I even remember photographs from *Lands and Peoples*
like the one of the knicker-clad hiker pausing to survey a
narrow pass in the Julian Alps.

Sometimes now I'll sit here at my desk, and maybe I'll
have a musical-instrument catalogue open and I'll notice
a fife, and that fife reminds me of bagpipes, and the pipes
make me think of Scotland, and I'll see those shaggy long-
horned cattle grazing on wild oats and beyond them a low
house of rough-hewn stone and heather-thatched roof and
beyond that a path that leads down the hill to a shingle
beach. And I see myself in that house wearing a woolen
suit and snap-brim cap, and if I keep thinking long enough,
I'll see a border collie asleep by the hearth. I can't help it.
I come from a long line of dreamers, and I guess I never
got it out of my system. My grandfather made it here from
Quebec when he was fourteen. He got a job repairing looms
in a Lowell mill and started himself a new life. My old
man planned on homesteading in Alaska back before the
war, but he married my mother instead.

Anyway, after high school I had less time to worry about
not being popular or brilliant, and so I was not as sad as
I'd been, and I quit writing poems. Until this thing with
Cliff, the worst I'd ever felt was the night that Mouse
McDermott's little sister Betty-Ann dumped me in front
of the Parkway Diner for this stocky Italian kid with a
Harley-Davidson. I was seventeen. Right after that I started

seeing Rosemary Houlihan, fell in love, and the rest, as they say, is history.

Funny thing was I'd gone through twelve years of school with Rosemary, and I'll bet we hadn't spoken more than three sentences to each other. I knew that her mother worked at the five-and-ten and that her father was dead. She missed the entire fourth grade with rheumatic fever but passed on to the fifth with the rest of us. She was always very quiet, just sort of stood around at recess, and she had terrific handwriting. A month or so after graduation, I saw her at the bus stop, said hello, told her I was on my way to a pops concert at the Auditorium, and, just like that, asked her if she'd like to go. That's how it started.

So how does a guy who wrote poetry and aced geography in school wind up running a small musical-instrument rental concern? You tell me. Things just happen sometimes. One thing leads to another, you know, and pretty soon there's another mouth to feed and so on. Anyway, that's not important. What is important is that my wife and I are happy after twenty-four years together. We still live in the old neighborhood. We've got this cottage, I guess you'd call it, over on Textile Avenue eight blocks or so from St. Veronica's Church. The house is eggshell-white with lilac shutters and has a screened-in veranda out front. I love it out there on summer nights with a cold brew, Sox on the radio, sheet lightning dancing in the sky. There's Rosemary and I and the two boys, Chuckie, thirteen, and Arthur, eleven. And there's Cliff Houlihan, my wife's older brother. Cliff came to live with us two years ago when his mother, God rest her soul, passed away. Three strokes in four days. Bang, bang, bang. We moved the boys in together and gave Cliff the other upstairs bedroom.

Cliff's no trouble at all. Keeps his room neat as a convent. He's got these amber rosary beads draped over his bedpost. And on the small pine nightstand by the bed is a cardboard-framed photo of his mother standing on the footbridge at Elm Park, shading her eyes from the sun with a gloved hand. Beside the photo lie the latest issues of *Reader's Digest* and *St. Anthony's Messenger.* The mahogany dresser has a large mirror attached, and wedged between the ebonized frame and the glass are a St. Jude prayer card and a small photo-booth snapshot of Cliff and his ex-girlfriend Kate Tivnan. They both look startled in the picture. Cliff says they were reaching down to press the start button when the flash surprised them.

Cliff was a paratrooper in Korea. He caught some shrapnel in his back, and hasn't been able to work steadily since. Once every other month he takes the bus into Boston to the VA hospital for a checkup, and that gives him a chance to see some of his old buddies from Southie. His disability checks don't amount to much, but then Cliff doesn't need much. All he ever buys for himself are those white socks with the two colored stripes at the top and white T-shirts. He has two pairs of slacks, a shiny gabardine pair that he wears to sleep in when it's chilly and a pair of khaki chinos that he wears outside the house. Rosemary's always telling Cliff that she'll let down the cuffs on his pants so the white socks won't show above his oxblood brogues, but Cliff tugs at his earlobe and asks what difference would that make.

The clothes are like his monastic habit. Cliff spent nearly a year at a Trappist abbey right after the war, and he still has some of the monk in him. He left the Trappists when the abbot told him to stop drinking. Cliff said he didn't see how whiskey interfered with his devotion to God. In fact, he told the abbot, it's less a distraction than shooting at Communists or running the monastery gift shop. Nonetheless, the abbot concluded that Cliff did not have the vocation.

So Cliff left the monastery, but he's continued to live austerely. He's simplified his life. And he still prays a lot. When you ask him what he's always thinking about, he's liable to say something like he's trying to solve the problem of being a mortal with immortal aspirations. He'll laugh about that, but you know he takes it seriously. I don't know anyone else quite like Cliff. Sometimes he'll inspire me, and I'll try to do like him, think about what he calls the desires of the soul and the demands of the body. But I'll hardly get started when I remember a back order of music stands or Chuckie's dentist appointment or something.

He wears his T-shirts backwards for some reason so that there's always a small white rectangle just below his Adam's apple. He wears a miraculous medal outside the shirt and a navy-blue cardigan buttoned to the breastbone. That's how he dresses every day. In the winter when he goes out, he'll put on this dappled tweed overcoat that once belonged to his father. The sleeves of the coat stop an inch above Cliff's wrists. He refuses to wear gloves or scarves or rubbers no matter how cold or sleety it gets. I suppose that's a monastic vestige, too. For a while there we had problems

with the boys wanting to dress like Uncle Cliffie, but I
finally got that straightened out one Sunday night with a
stern "Because I told you so."

It always smells like Brylcreem in Cliff's room and a
few feet out into the hallway. Cliff brushes the hair straight
back from his forehead so it looks like a helmet. His hair
used to be ink-black when we were younger. We called
him Blackie, in fact. But now it's that dull iron color of
horned pout. And he's got these flakes of eczema all along
the hairline that set off the pinkness of his face and fore-
head. Cliff drinks, as I said, but his theory is if you can
keep your hair combed, you're not drunk.

Every morning Cliff goes to Mass at St. Veronica's. He
and this old Lithuanian woman are usually the only two
at six-thirty Mass, unless there's a snowstorm. Then I give
Cliff a lift and I'm the third. Cliff has always been reli-
gious. He was an altar boy as a kid, a good one, too. After
Sunday Masses he sold newspapers from a homemade
stand outside the church. Then one Sunday in Lent, Mon-
signor Reilly caught Cliff drinking wine from the cruet
and replacing it with holy water from the font in the ves-
tibule. He was asked to hand in his cassock and surplice.

Until about a year ago Cliff had this girlfriend that I
mentioned. She had strawberry-blond hair and blue eyes.
Cliff and Kate dated for seventeen years. They met when
Cliff put in some time as a school crossing guard and Kate
was teaching eighth-grade English at East Middle School.
Every Tuesday and Friday night they'd meet at Moyni-
han's Tavern, sit at a booth, and talk until midnight. Moy-
nihan's attracts a neighborhood crowd. Some of the regulars
have been drinking there for thirty or more years and sit

on stools their fathers sat in before them. The old hard-
wood floor has been tiled, but little else has changed. There
are Venetian blinds on the front windows, yellow lamps at
each booth. Over the bar there's a photograph of old Davy
Moynihan shaking hands with James Michael Curley.

Usually by the end of their night, Kate would end up
reciting poems to Cliff. She could recite poems for hours
without repeating a line. Cliff was delighted to sit and lis-
ten. He especially liked those Irish love poems about west-
ern wind, blood-red wine, fair-skinned lasses, and like that.
And then on Saturdays they'd drive Kate's car out to the
AOH Hall on the lake and eat steamers and listen to Irish
music.

The first week of every August they would rent Room
134 at the Bayberry Lodge in Dennisport. Those were the
only nights they ever spent together under the same roof,
Cliff told me. Every year Cliff would return from his week
at the beach as pale as when he left, but wearing sun-
glasses and some zany wide-brimmed hat with a minia-
ture beer can attached to it. Kate would be pink except for
her peeling shoulders and nose, and she smelled of
Noxzema and would walk very gingerly for several days.
On their first night back to Moynihan's, they'd wear
matching souvenir sweatshirts which read "U.S. Olympic
Drinking Team" or "I'm with Stupid" or something like
that.

Anyway, Kate finally married the assistant principal of
East Middle School, an Italian guy named Buffone or
Baroni, I forget which. My guess is that Kate just couldn't
wait any longer for Cliff to make up his mind. Either that
or he told her he was happy with the arrangement they

had and she wasn't. First I knew anything was wrong was when I heard Rosemary raise her voice to Cliff out in the kitchen. "Why don't you do something about it, for heaven's sakes?" she was saying. "What do you expect the woman to do, Cliff?" Anyway, Cliff went to the wedding reception at the Elks and wished the newlyweds all the luck. When he came home, he told me, "Life goes on," and went to his room.

We try to eat supper at five. It's the only time that the family can all get together. Once in a while I'll get tied up in traffic or one of the boys will have music lessons, but usually we manage to sit down at five. The boys tell us everything that happened at school, how they did on this or that test, how much money was collected for the missions, when hockey tryouts will be, and so on. Rosemary fills us in on the neighborhood news—who owes who money, whose son was promoted at the Shawmut Bank, and like that. Cliff will ask about my day and make bowling or movie plans with Arthur and Chuckie for the weekend.

Then after supper the boys hit the books for an hour—family rule—Rosemary and I do the dishes, and Cliff empties the rubbish. At six-fifteen sharp Cliff walks the two blocks to Moynihan's. On his way he stops at Battista's Market for a pack of Salem Lights, an instant lottery ticket, and the *Herald*, which he folds lengthwise and slips into his coat pocket.

At Moynihan's, Cliff sits at the bar with one or two of the regulars, guys he grew up with, and they watch TV on the big screen—usually nature shows or Benny Hill, or the Celtics if they're on. Cliff will drink five shots of Jameson's and a half-dozen pints of ale, and at nine-thirty he'll eat one pickled egg and a Slim Jim. At ten he comes home, drinks a glass of warm milk, reads the *Herald* at the kitchen table, brushes his teeth, combs his hair, says good night to my wife and me, and heads upstairs for bed.

But this past Monday it was five and Cliff wasn't home, and I was concerned because Mondays mean corned beef and cabbage at our house, and that's Cliff's favorite meal.

"This isn't like Cliff," I said as we sat down to eat.

Chuckie said grace and then Rosemary said, "Haven't you noticed that Cliff's been on a diet?"

I hadn't, but I did recall that he told me he was cutting back on eggs and ale; he'd developed a sensitive stomach.

"He's being shy about it," Rosemary said, "but it's beginning to show. His face is thinner already, and he's even looking younger."

"You don't suppose he has another girlfriend?" I said. The boys said they sure hoped not.

Arthur said maybe Cliff missed the bus back from the VA. I had forgotten it was his VA day. If he missed the three forty-five bus, he'd be rolling into town about six and would probably head right for Moynihan's. So after I dried the dishes, I called the bar, but Cliff hadn't shown up. Later, Rosemary insisted on calling the police. The cops told her that a person wasn't missing until he was gone for twenty-four hours, and no, they had no reports of any bus accident. We went to sleep at eleven, later than usual, and left the back porch light on.

In the morning, Rosemary called the VA hospital and got the terrible news. Cliff has cancer. Cancer of the pancreas complicated with cirrhosis. Rosemary just stood there, so I took the phone. With radiation therapy, the doctor told me, Cliff has at best maybe six months to live. Without it—a month. He said they found the cancer two weeks ago during Cliff's routine annual physical.

"You didn't know?" the doctor said.

"No."

"Well, you need to. Cliff's going to need more care than we can give him here. You'll have to make arrangements."

"He hasn't come home."

"He left here yesterday about two, I'd say. He was upset, of course."

"Of course."

"That's not unusual."

"I don't imagine it is."

Rosemary took out the ironing board and began to reiron the living-room drapes. She always cleans when she's upset. I went to work leaving instructions for her to call me the second she heard from Cliff. A light snow and icy roads slowed the traffic to a crawl, and I had plenty of time to think. I tried to be logical, tried to think like Cliff. Where would he have disappeared to? But what happened was I kept thinking about what I would do if I were Cliff, and I knew I was going to die. And I kept fixing on this image of the way Cliff always winks at me over his coffee cup every morning when I leave for work and says, "Be sweet, Johnny."

At work, I sat at my desk, and all I could think about was Cliff: Cliff at the supper table smiling at one of Arthur's bad jokes; Cliff lying on the sofa reading a detective novel; Cliff sitting with Kate at Moynihan's. And that's when I realized I knew where Cliff was. I called Rosemary and told her. I said I'd have Cliff home as soon as I could. I switched off the answering machine, put the "Closed" sign on the door, and left.

The Bayberry Lodge is off Sea Street about a block from the ocean. Cliff was out back by the tarp-covered pool sitting at a white metal table under a Cinzano umbrella. He wore the green woolen Celtics hat that the boys had given him for Christmas and wraparound Foster Grants. "Thanks for coming to get me," he said. Cliff took off the glasses, reached in his pocket, and pulled out a stack of Bayberry Lodge postcards. "I've been busy writing."

"Cliff, I . . ."

"Have a drink with me, Johnny."

I sat down and Cliff pulled a fifth of Jameson's from his other coat pocket and passed it to me. "He hasn't made it easy for us," Cliff said. "But He has provided consolation." He smiled.

"Cliff, we can get you another doctor, some treatment. I mean, this thing can be licked."

Cliff smiled and shook his head. "I'm going to die. This tumor is the size of an eggplant."

"Cliff, you can't just give up."

"I'm not giving up. I'm dying."

I swallowed more whiskey and slid the bottle back to Cliff. I usually don't drink the hard stuff, but this tasted warm and necessary. Cliff sipped and said, "You know what I'll miss most, Johnny? I'll miss what's going to happen after I'm gone. Do you know what I mean? Like Frank

Sinatra. I've been thinking about him a lot this morning. Seems like I've been listening to him all my life. He's had his ups and downs like all the rest of us, right? Well, I want to know what happens next. Does he make a comeback or die in a plane crash or what? I feel like I'm missing the end of the movie."

"But you came here because of Kate."

"Sure, we loved it here."

"You know she still cares about you."

"I was afraid to get married. I got all mixed up somewhere. How did you do it, Johnny?"

"What?"

"Get married. Have a family. All of that."

"I never thought about it really." I stared past Cliff's shoulder to the motel office and tried to smell the ocean.

"I didn't have any confidence," he said. "So I went to the monastery. I told myself if I had no distractions, if I kept it simple, I could control my life."

"That makes sense."

"Not anymore."

I wanted to tell Cliff that I would miss him. That his sister and his nephews would miss him. That he had made a difference. That he was kind and smart and cared about important things that I was too busy and too stupid to think about. I couldn't talk, though. I felt suddenly cold. I fumbled for the car keys in my pocket.

"I can remember as a kid wanting to be somebody important. Somebody you'd read about in newspapers or maybe even the encyclopedia. But I didn't know how. They didn't teach us that in school, did they, Johnny?"

I shook my head and took another swig.

"I didn't want to be a soldier. I knew that much. Made no sense the way they changed the rules. You're seventeen and killing's a sin. You're eighteen, it's heroic. I didn't think they could have it both ways. So I spent seven months in Korea scared to death. I tell you, Johnny, I was glad when I got hit." He felt his back where, I knew, a kidney was missing and metal was lodged. "But listen to me. I'm preaching."

"What did you want to be, Cliff?"

"I wanted to be an explorer. Isn't that funny? I wanted to discover the sources of rivers and conquer mountain ranges, and it turns out I can't even get out of my own neighborhood without a bus-route map."

I didn't think it was funny. I thought it was sad, like everything else in the universe at that moment there in the back of a nearly deserted motel on a darkening winter afternoon. Snowflakes drifted by our faces. Our bottle was empty. "Cliff?"

"What?"

"Are you afraid?"

"No. The fear's gone."

I said, "Call Kate, will you."

"Give me a few minutes, Johnny, and then we'll go home."

I imagined Cliff wanted to say goodbye to Room 134 and to the smell of Noxzema and the echo of Kate's melodic voice. I sat in the idling car, started the defrost. Hot air blew into my eyes and flushed my face. What would we do with Cliff's room? I could put maps on the wall, all those *Geographic* maps I have stored in the attic. And photos of exotic places. I could plan trips up there, trips Rose-

mary and I could take when the boys are on their own and
I have someone to manage the store. Why was I thinking
like that? I was planning my life without Cliff, and here
he was in his father's overcoat walking toward me across
the motel parking lot. We'll have to buy him a suit, I real-
ized. We can't bury him in a T-shirt and cardigan.

We started home. I drove the old roads. I didn't want
the ride to end. Cliff stared out the window most of the
way. When you've traveled to the Cape as often as Cliff
has—seventeen years' worth—then probably every bend
in the road, every roadside stand, carried a memory with
it. And he was playing it all back one last time. I stopped
at a package store in Bridgewater and bought a bottle of
Jameson's. We opened it there in the lot and quietly shared
the whiskey.

Cliff told me that he had rented Room 134 for the first
week in August. "I guess I'm entitled to a final sentimen-
tal gesture."

"Come on, Cliff, don't talk like that."

"Johnny, you know that old woman in Mass every
morning?"

"Mrs. Maironis?"

"Right. She's eighty-six, she's a widow, and she worries
about me. She'll be upset when she doesn't see me at
church. I want you to talk to her, okay?"

"Sure, Cliff."

So now Cliff's back at the hospital for treatment. We
don't know if he'll be coming home. I'm here at work writ-
ing this down. Cliff's problems have me thinking about
my own life. Things have just sort of happened. My job,
for example. I don't particularly like drums and bugles. I

hate martial music, but here I am, sole proprietor of Paramount Music, Inc. I work at my job, pay my taxes, keep up my property, tend to the needs of my wife and children, and pray when I can afford the time.

I want to leave. I'd like to go to that crofter's cottage, the one with the border collie. I want sea, sky, and solitude. And on long summer nights, to walk the gravel path past the unthatched still, past the old limekiln, through fields of deergrass and heather. I'll follow the dry stone wall down the moor to the sea and gather whelks for eating and kelp for cooking. I'll scythe wildflowers for hay, cut peat from bogs, net fish in the sound, and trek to town on market days.

I called Cliff last night from Moynihan's and told him this. I figured it was something a dying man could understand. He did. He told me to take the family and go. Not to think about it, just to leave as soon as possible. He even offered me all the money in his bank account. "Your life could really be like that dream," he said. "You'd be doing it for the both of us." When I asked him what would happen if Rosemary didn't like the idea, he said I could go alone for a little while. I told him I'd miss the boys. He got angry. He said, "If you don't want to go, don't." And he hung up on me.

On the way to work this morning, I stopped by St. Veronica's. In the vestibule I met Mrs. Maironis and told her that Cliff was very sick, that he wouldn't be coming to church for a while. "I'll light a candle for Mr. Houlihan," she told me. She blessed herself with holy water and went in to Mass.

I took Cliff's usual pew beneath the stained-glass win-

dow of St. Jude. I stared at the back of this old woman in
a black cloth coat and wondered whom or what she prayed
for morning after morning. Was she ever astonished to
find herself alone in this dark sanctuary? Did she lift her
eyes one morning to the vaulted ceiling and notice the ray
of light from the clerestory window and remember once
dancing with a splendid young suitor or weaving a garland
of violets through her long red hair?

The Sanctus bell rang. Father Farrell elevated the host;
Mrs. Maironis bowed her head. I checked my watch: six
forty-five. The boys would just be getting out of bed. And
on my Scottish island it was nearly noon, and solitary men
sat on limestone hills and stared into the sea.

I said a prayer for Cliff and went to work.

SURVEYORS

THERE WERE SIX rows of twelve tomato plants each. Each plant was pruned to a single stem and tied with ribbons of plaid flannel to sturdy five-foot-tall hickory stakes. Training the vines made the weeding and the liming easier, my grandfather said. It exposed the fruit to more sunlight, which produced a richer color and a sweeter taste. Glossy, elliptical Earlianas bunched in clusters on tender-vined plants. He also grew Burbanks with thick, solid skins and juicy flesh. These were his favorites. The Bonny Bests were brilliantly red, flattened and globular, and often swelled in size to six inches across. He gave these away like trophies to his friends.

The littered, overweeded lot next to his apartment building had become my grandfather's tomato garden. And every July evening in 1953, the year of the polio epidemic in Massachusetts when I was five, he and I would finish supper and sit out on the grass beside the cinder driveway and watch the garden.

He was a housepainter and a difficult man at times. Whenever he wore one of his two suits he drank too much. Every time he drank too much, he took off his leather belt and strapped somebody. One night after returning from a nephew's wedding in Lowell, he locked his wife and children out of the house, fired four .22-caliber bullets into the walnut body of a console radio, and hid all of the food from the icebox under his bed. That was before I arrived for the summer, and before the garden was planted.

I carried his green glass bottle of warm Tadcaster ale like a chalice to our grass seats. He wore a beige straw hat with a narrow downturned brim and a seersucker band. He surveyed the garden, his green eyes inspecting each plant in turn. He stood up, picked his teeth with the edge of a matchbook, took off the hat, and fanned his face. His thin chestnut hair was graying at the temples even then. The pleated brown-flannel trousers were zipped but unbuttoned and were held up by olive Y-back suspenders that followed the white paths of his T-shirt straps over his large shoulders. I see the tomatoes for us, he said, and flopped away in his cordovan slip-ons to gather our dessert.

My tomato smelled of linseed oil from the touch of his short thick fingers. He drew a yellow shaker, shaped like a tiny ear of corn, from his pocket, took his first taste of tomato, and sprinkled salt into the bite.

He told me the Depression story. How he had lost his home, a seven-room cottage that he had built himself with the weekend help of six of his fifteen brothers. The red house sat on a shaded avenue away from the factories. It had a backyard large enough for two pear trees, a rhododendron bush, and a small vegetable garden. He wiped his stiff-bristled mustache with a handkerchief and then dried a thin pink river of tomato juice meandering down my wrist. That's why, he said, he hadn't deposited one dime in a bank for twenty-three years. That's why his savings were stashed like memories where no one else could find them—locked in steel boxes and hidden in the secret cavities of floors and walls and ceilings.

Told me how when the bank foreclosed and he was out of work, he moved his family to a fifteen-dollar-a-month flat and wondered how he'd feed six kids. He built a two-story pigeon coop and raised homers. Taste like chicken, he said. He set squirrel traps, planted tomatoes and beans, and fished for calico bass and horned pout in the quarry pond at the old brickyards. That's when he smuggled whiskey on the trains from Montreal to Worcester. He wanted me to know that I would not be saved by my possessions. It's not what you have, he said, but how you are. The bastards can't take that from you.

The fussy old French priests in this parish are as crooked as ward bosses, he said. Every one of them. Joe McCarthy

is the only politician in this country who cares about poor
people, he said. You watch, we're going to make him
President.

We had seen Ted Williams play baseball for the first
time that summer on my grandfather's new nineteen-inch
Motorola television. My grandfather was fascinated by the
explosive grace of Mr. Williams's brilliant swing and by
the way he defied both pitcher and probability by always
taking the first strike. Even the great DiMaggio could not
do that. DiMaggio needed three strikes. That's the art, my
grandfather said, giving a strike to the pitcher.

As my grandfather talked and I listened, two men stepped
down from the cab of a maroon pickup. One man nodded
to my grandfather. The smaller one slid a tripod from the
truck bed and lifted it to his shoulder. No, it's not a tele-
scope, he said. It's a transit. The men are surveyors. They're
here to measure the property. He sent me to the house for
another bottle of ale. When I returned he was talking with
the young man in the Sanforized green jumpsuit. The man
wore a Yankee baseball cap on the back of his head so that
the bill pointed skyward. He stood near the edge of the
garden between rows of Burbanks and held a striped range
pole with his right hand. When he blushed at something
my grandfather said, he looked like another tomato plant.
They're going to build a house, my grandfather said. They
start tomorrow. But it's our garden, I said. But it's not our
land, he said.

In the morning he dressed for work in his white bib
overalls, white shirt, and white Pratt & Lambert painter's
hat, and sat quietly at the kitchen table, drinking coffee.
He heard the horn and walked outside and told his friend

Studley to go on without him; he would catch a bus to work later. He carried a galvanized tub to the garden and began a final harvest. By the time the flatbed truck delivered the bulldozer and its driver to the lot, he had filled and unloaded the tub three times. He gave me a grocery bag from Candella's market and told me to fill it with tomatoes and give them to the driver. We have enough tomatoes. I refused. He's going to kill our plants, I said. The man is doing his job, he said.

We took our grass seats and watched the bulldozer rip the land and crush the plants into the rocky soil until there was nothing left to look at.

THE WAY THAT
WATER ENTERS
STONE

SOME MORNINGS I wake up, stare at the ceiling a
moment to get my bearings, and realize I'm alive and don't
have a toothache. And sometimes that's enough. I get up,
grab my pen, my clipboard and log, hop in the Checker,
and shoot over to the Alice and the Hat Diner for coffee.
I'll buy the paper or maybe bring along whatever book I'm
into and sit there in a booth and read. But other mornings,
I need more wisdom than I went to bed with to get me up.

This one morning, I woke up—I live in the Royal Hotel,
upstairs from Thelma's Cut 'n' Curl—and stared at the
ceiling and saw that brown water stain in the shape of

Australia. I located Perth, Sydney, Alice Springs, and right there where Ayers Rock would be. This was nothing new. I was always looking up at Australia. I looked across at my chinos folded over the hot plate, scratched at my crotch, stretched my legs taut. This was one of those dangerous mornings when I had questions I wanted answers to.

Like I wanted to know what I thought I was doing hanging on to my wife, Donna. Why did I hope she'd come back one more time? Why did I even want her to? Here I was with my life on hold again, imagining things would somehow be different the next time. The first time Donna left me I stayed in bed for three days. That was in 1976. I was a wreck. I was also a junior high school science teacher. I should have moved out of that trailer, gotten away from her mirrors and nylons, from the residue of her perfumes, from the refrigerator where she taped the note: "Dear Robert, I need time to sort things out. I'll write from Marblehead, explain everything. Your D."

Instead, I went into therapy. What Dr. Parella and I figured out after sixteen weeks was that I had two dreams— to travel to some of the natural wonders that I talked about in class, to get out of my books and into the world, that, and perhaps a less realistic dream: to live happily ever after with my wife. Dr. Parella pointed out, delicately, I might add, that those dreams were, in fact, not dreams at all, but delusions. I was to forget Donna, he said, forget the exploration, plant my feet firmly on the ground, step out and meet other women, get a master's degree, and work my way up to vice principal or something.

I didn't want to remember any more of that period of my life, so I stared back up at Australia. I imagined myself

in the outback, tracing a fault line through the Northern
Territory. My Land Rover's broken down—I don't know,
fan belt snapped or something. I'm out of Foster's. It's
dark and I haven't enough brush to keep the fire burning
through the night. I hear the maniacal barking of a pack
of dingoes setting off for the night's hunt. I was, as you
see, determined to keep Donna out of my thoughts, but
suddenly, what had been this mountain range in Queens-
land began to look like Donna's face and hair. That lux-
urious red hair, those green, Aegean eyes, that smile I'd
die for. What's the use? I heard a knock at my door. I
ignored it.

I read a book about chaos once, about how a butterfly
flaps his wings on a peony in central China in June and
the tiny disturbance of air displaces other swirls of air and
eventually causes it to rain in Scranton in August. Each
thing you do, no matter how trivial, will be the cause of
everything else you do for the rest of your life. So that
afternoon at the Jersey Bar when Donna sipped her mint
tea and told me she was afraid to end up planted in front
of the TV with a pack of Chesterfields like her mother,
and I told her then she should do what she needed to to
make her life exciting and rich, maybe at that moment I
sentenced myself to a long-suffering wedlock. Just my luck
to be in love with a wife who's in search of stimulation
and abundance, romance and the grand passion. It's not
the man in each affair, but the opportunity to reveal her-
self all over again to someone new and intensely willing
that sweeps her off her feet. Some consolation. Of course,
I'm smart enough to know that the man in Scranton can

get in out of the storm. Almost smart enough to know that this time Donna might not be coming back.

One thing I like about Donna is the way she launches into enthusiasms. She keeps hoping she'll find the life she's good at. She'll take chances. She has courage and passion, but no tenderness. Nothing stops her. I'm just not sure what it is that drives her. At times I think I understand her, how desperate the flatness of marriage must make her feel, say, or how easy it might be to confess to a stranger. Other times I don't think I even know her. Like once she told me that behind the sun is the real sun. I said the one in the sky was real enough for me—keeps me warm, shows up on time, makes all those nice colors. She shook her head. I said, well, what the hell do you want me to do with that information, Donna? That was the night she told me our problem was we got married on April 30.

"What's that supposed to mean?"

"April 30. Beltane."

"I give up."

"Witches' holy day, Robert. Bad day to begin a relation-ship."

"So that kind of lets you off the hook then, doesn't it?"

Another knock at my door. I rolled out of bed. "Com-ing!"

"It's me, Robert. It's Martin Charbonneau."

I opened the door. Martin stood in our grimy hallway wearing his light blue pajamas. The hallway reeked of whatever curious chemical it is that curls hair. "Come on in, Martin."

Martin held his arms stiffly at his sides as if standing at

attention. He opened, then clenched his fists. "Louise . . ." he said.

"Martin, you've been crying."

"I . . . can't . . . f-find . . ."

"Please, Martin, come in." I held his two shoulders to stop their trembling. He bit his lip.

"I can't find Louise."

"Let me get ready, and then I'll help you look." I hurried down the hall to shave and wash. When I got back, Martin had curled to sleep on my unmade bed.

Martin had lost his wife again. He and Louise live down the hall from me in 4B, a two-room flat with a bathroom and kitchenette. I knew she must be at one of the three places we always looked for her. Nevertheless, Martin could never remember where it was she wandered off to, and anyway, he'd have gotten lost if he went after her. First, we'd check the children's room at the public library. If she wasn't there she'd be sitting on a bench at the Amtrak station or in a pew at Notre Dame Church. Sometimes she'd sit in the dark there and stare up at the splashes of color from the stained-glass windows. Other times she'd light all the votive candles in the baptistery. One time she caught her mitten and the sleeve of her jacket on fire and ran screaming out onto Franklin Street, waving her arm above her head. This kid, who at first thought Louise was playing Statue of Liberty, had the fortunate presence of mind to smother the flames with his jacket.

Martin is from a small town somewhere in Maine and doesn't know how he wound up in central Massachusetts.

He *thinks* he's been here most of his life. He remembers
that he met Louise at the Belchertown State Hospital a
couple of years ago, that they liked each other, and that
they got married. Martin is forty-three, Louise twenty-one,
and they were certainly blessed to have found each other.
They are both moderately retarded and have difficulty
dealing with unusual situations. This worried me. And it
worried their social worker, this guy named Jakubiak, even
more. The first time I ran into Jakubiak at Martin's, he
had a carton of condoms under his arm.

"These are for you," he told Martin.

"Not my birthday."

"It's not a gift, Martin."

"No thanks."

"What I mean is I, we, the Department . . . What the
hell am I saying?"

"I don't know."

"You and Louise use these when you, you know, make
love."

"Oh."

"You understand then?"

"No." Martin was definite.

So Jakubiak opened an illustrated pamphlet, smoothed
it flat on the kitchen table, and cleared his throat. Since
Martin couldn't read the instructions, Jakubiak did. When
he finished, he looked at Martin for some reaction. "Do
you have any questions?"

Martin shook his head.

"Do you know what to do?"

Martin smiled. "No."

Jakubiak looked over to me. I smiled and looked at the

linoleum floor. He said out loud, but to himself, "I've got no business doing this. I don't care if it is my job," excused himself, nodded to me, and walked out the door.

I liked Jakubiak right away and later persuaded him to give it another try. This time he had a visiting nurse talk to Louise about the pill. So Louise got her monthly dispenser but either she'd divvy the pills evenly with Martin, or else she'd forget to take them, or would conscientiously take a week's worth on Sunday morning, that sort of thing. That's how Louise got pregnant, and that's when she started running off and Martin started losing her.

"There she is, Martin," I said. We had just walked into the crowded station. She was eating popcorn and watching the armchair television in the Amtrak waiting room. "Go get her. I'll drive you two home."

This was the fifth time in three weeks I'd rescued Martin and Louise. The child inside didn't make her sick or rose her cheeks with the blush of motherhood; it made her as restless as a cat hunting for a place to have her litter.

As I drove them home, Martin and Louise sat in the back of the cab eating popcorn and chatting about the game show she'd been watching. I sat spouseless up front, imagining Donna relaxed on a sofa in some airy living room somewhere, Sunday *Globe* folded on her lap, holding a coffee cup to her lips with both hands, smiling at what the voice from the den is telling her. I try to make this Donna get up, walk to the window, think about me, but that waxy voice has her attention. Here it is my own reverie, but the characters ignore me, do just what they feel like. How does that happen?

Donna left me the first time for her psychology professor from the college, who was opening a place called the
Center for Human Potential up on the North Shore. She
had found his ministry more compelling, I suppose, than
my own—teaching earth science to ninth-graders. When
she came home on a Saturday afternoon some three months
later, I was lying in front of the tube watching candlepin
bowling. "Donna, my God, where have . . ."

"Robert," she interrupted, "Robert, let's forget what
happened. Today is the first day of the rest of our lives."
She knelt beside me, touched my chest with her hand.

I tried to say something.

"Sssh." Donna put her finger to my lips. "Don't cry,
Robert. Your baby is back."

"I can't believe this."

She kissed me. "We won't let what's happened come
between us, will we?"

"Well, what happened?"

"We can't live in the past, Robert. I've learned that. The
past is a foreign country." She lay down on top of me.
"Make me happy," she said.

The first day, I thought.

Donna showed me the new dulcimer Barry, the professor, had given her as a going-away gift. She played "Go
Tell Aunt Rhody" and said she had decided to be a folksinger. So while I graded science tests, she made the rounds
of the local clubs, and within a month was singing with a
string band called One Hand Clapping at antinuke rallies.

The band belonged to something called the Clamshell Alliance which was determined to shut down the Seabrook power plant up in New Hampshire. When I intimated that I might like to join the cause, Donna counterintimated that I was encroaching on her territory. "Can't I ever have anything of my own!" I think was how she put it.

Donna, the string band, and about two thousand others were arrested blockading the plant, and because they refused bail, spent three weeks in the Seabrook Armory. They didn't stop the construction, but did provide fodder for barrages of pity in the teachers' lounge at Chandler Junior High. Robert's-wife-is-at-it-again kind of talk. The women brought me casseroles. The other male teachers in the Science Department asked why I allowed Donna to get involved with politics in the first place. It was the beginning of my end at Chandler. When Donna got released, she told me she needed space. That meant she needed Chris, one of the dozen or so flannel-shirted guitarists she knew, who had beguiled her with moral certitude and charmed her with three chords. Improbable as it sounds, I missed her.

You know, the thing that drives me crazy is that I had it all one time—wife, oak furniture, a white Persian cat, a job turning into a career, families over to dinner, color television, a list of errands taped to the fridge, a bartender at the neighborhood pub who knew my first name and usual drink. I was normal. And now what? I live in this musty hotel alone, with an uncertain future and a past that seeps into everything I do like water into stone. You know how water does, class, I told them, it trickles through crevices, runs along channels and gathers itself in pools, stands there. Come the cold, it freezes, expands, cracks the rock, then spills through new fractures, all the time wearing at the stone, collects again, freezes. From the outside, nothing seems to have changed, but within, the damage mounts and maybe the whole formation collapses. Thus mountains are razed to plains.

These memories of Donna have the strength and patience of water seeking its level, leveling me. And there's nothing the stone can do.

Louise was due in a matter of weeks. Jakubiak had this other client who'd just had her tubes knotted after eight kids, and she was tossing out one of her cribs, so he asked if I'd help him move it up to Martin's. On the way over, he told me he was worried.

"They won't be able to care for the baby."

"Oh, they'll do okay."

"They can't read."

"I know."

"They can't even be trusted with medication for the baby."

I hadn't thought of that.

"And this crib. If we don't put it together, it'll sit there."

"So, we'll put it together."

"What kind of future will this kid have?"

"What do you propose?"

Jakubiak sat quietly. He took off his glasses. By then we were parked outside his client's building. "The right thing."

"For whom?"

He breathed on the lenses, then wiped them with his
tie.

We hefted the crib up to Martin's, assembled it, and
rolled it to a corner of the living room. Martin and Louise
sat holding hands on the green loveseat and watched us. I
remembered how Donna and I would watch the Late Show
cuddled on our couch, how she'd fall asleep with her head
in my lap. Her mouth would be open and she'd drool.
While Jakubiak ran down to Zayre's for sheets and what-
not, I sat around with Martin and Louise. I sat on the floor
by the coffee table and made small talk. I asked them if
they'd settled on a name for the child yet. Martin just stared
at me like maybe I was a hypnotist's watch or something.
Louise thought the baby came with a name, which, if you
think about it, is a pretty mystical notion. Maybe we do
come with names. Or should. But that's not what I told
them. I told them why not pick a name they liked from a
television show. That's what they do mostly, watch TV. If
it was a boy, they agreed they'd name the baby Mr. Wiz-
ard.

Donna and I talked about having kids twice. I hoped
that motherhood would settle her down. Her arrangement
with Chris had lasted nearly three months, but then one
day she was home and wanted to start over, and this time,
she said, her heart was in it. That's when I brought up the
idea of starting a family. "Let's take care of each other
first," she said. She figured she'd be ready to consider
motherhood when she was thirty-five or so. She got into
natural foods and herbs instead. Donna and a handful of

others from her night school class spent their Saturday mornings foraging through vacant lots and city parks for pokeweed, currants, snow mushrooms, and such. They'd collect the food, then go to the teacher's apartment and have themselves a green feast. My strategy has always been to encourage Donna's enthusiasms, to contort myself to her will and whim. I loved her.

We had a chart of 127 useful herbs on our bedroom wall. It listed the history of each herb, the medicinal and culinary uses of each, with dosages and preparations and . recipes. That spring we gathered nettle and cooked it up. If you boil it for twenty minutes, you get a dish of slightly bitter greens. If you boil it for two hours, you end up with this elixir guaranteed to keep your hair from falling out. Donna worried about my thinning hair. She brewed dandelion coffee for my thermos each morning and made a decent "lemonade" from sumac berries. All in all, though, Donna felt urban plants were too tainted with industrial pollutants to be very beneficial. She began talking about moving to the country.

She would sit on the couch with our cat, Boz, and read Burpee seed catalogues and Strout Realty listings. This was a difficult concept for me, the idea of owning acres of rocks and pine cones and weedy bottomland. But Donna was so excited that I began to appreciate the idea. I figured I could learn about plows and tillers later. I could wear those clunky boots, ax firewood, rock by an iron stove, suffer a little.

We were going back to nature in a big way. Donna had become inexplicably struck with a seizure of domestic longing. We were going to buy a farmhouse in New

Hampshire. She wanted a spacious kitchen, she said, and a studio to do crafts. And, Robert, she said, when we're settled in, we're going to start having kids. She even told me the names of the first five: Caitlin, Mark, Benjamin, Rachel, and Evan. Here at last we would do what we set out to do at our wedding: raise a proper family and live together happily ever after. My patience had paid off, I thought, relieved.

It was a sleety, windy Saturday morning, I remember, at the end of November. I was sitting at the card table in the parlor typing up a test on soil erosion when Donna came home from the library with a book on mushroom cultivation and another on candle making. She curled up on the couch with an afghan over her legs, the cat nestled at the back of her knees, purring. "I'm thinking of becoming a midwife," she said. I didn't hear her, so she repeated it.

"That's very nice, dear," I said.

"I'd have to go to school. In New York. We'll have to put off the farm for a while."

I was puzzled. "If that's what you want," I said. It was the wrong thing to say.

Donna slapped her book shut. The cat dove across the coffee table and scrambled behind the stereo cabinet. "You don't want to do this, do you?"

"What?"

"Any of it. You'll go along with anything."

What could I say?

"Well, I don't appreciate being patronized. I don't need it from you or anyone else."

I said, "Donna, you're supposed to do things for people you love. I'm not patronizing you."

So you know what she said? She said, "Don't pull that moral superiority bullshit on me, Robert. I'm not in ninth grade. And anyway, what the hell do you know above love?"

"Honey, calm down."

"Tell me! What do you know?"

I felt like I'd been rattled out of reverie by a teacher's voice, been caught staring out the window in history class. "What?"

"You heard me."

I thought I could tell her what I knew about love if I could just still my nerves and think. I'd tell her love is the gravity that holds your life together or love is imagination, it makes anything possible, or something like that. But I wasn't sure I was right. I hesitated.

"You don't love me," she said. "You love being married."

She walked into the kitchen and turned on the radio. She called her girlfriend and cried into the phone. Later, she packed two suitcases, called a cab, and moved to Boston. It's been nearly a year now. She got a job working for Barry, who was by then directing the state's program on abused and exploited children.

Speaking of children, that Monday I simplified my life: I flunked every student who took the science test. And I continued to flunk the entire ninth grade for the remainder of the term despite parental objections and administrative reprimands. After the school department psychologist spoke with me, I was relieved of my duties. I took a settle-

ment, broke the lease on our third-floor apartment, gave
the furniture to Catholic Charities, bought a used taxi from
Arrow Cab, and moved here to the Royal. Don't ask me
why.

Louise delivered a seven-pound-six-ounce baby girl at
City Hospital early on Thanksgiving morning and then
watched the Macy's parade in her room with Martin, Jak-
ubiak, and me. While admiring all those giant balloons,
Louise came up with a name for her daughter: Minnie.
Without the "Mouse" sounded better, I said. As far as
anyone knew, Minnie Charbonneau was the only infant
who had ever lived at the Royal Hotel. This was quite an
adjustment for the older residents, many of whom were
bothered by the baby's crying through the night. Even with
four floors of rattling, banging radiators, you could hear
the baby scream. There were several nights those first few
weeks that Martin scuttled down the hall to my room with
the baby and asked me to make it stop. It seemed when-
ever Minnie cried too loudly, Louise, thinking it was her
fault, locked herself in the bathroom.

On those nights, Minnie slept in my opened, towel-lined
vinyl suitcase by the side of the bed. While Martin spoke
to the bottle of formula warming on the hotplate, I'd listen
to the drone of the traffic on Front Street and the murmur
of Minnie's breathing. She had Martin's dark hair, nar-
row blue eyes, and startled expression. I enjoyed her visits.

Then, a few weeks later, I got a call from Jakubiak while
I was having a pepper steak at the diner. His voice sounded
panicked. Louise and the baby hadn't been at home when

he showed up with a nurse for their regular appointment. Martin didn't know where they'd gone. Martin forgets, I told him, trying to sound reassuring. I said sure, I'd check the usual places. When I did spot Louise, I had a fare and couldn't stop to chat. She was coming down the steps of Notre Dame carrying the bundle swaddled in a brown blanket. I breathed a sigh of relief. "Go home, Louise," I yelled out the window. She waved at me. I stopped as long as I could without holding up traffic at the next intersection until I saw her turn down Front Street on her way home.

It was an hour or so before I could get to a pay phone and ring up Jakubiak at the number he'd given me.

"I sent her home," I said.

"Then you haven't heard?"

"Heard what?"

"This nun at Notre Dame was dusting the altar when she heard a baby cry."

"Don't tell me."

"The baby was in the creche being watched over by three plaster magi. The nun thought it was a miracle. She fainted and fell into the manger. The noise alerted Father Scollen. He called the cops."

"It was Minnie."

"She'll be in the hospital overnight for observation, but she seems fine."

"What about the baby? I saw it in her arms."

Louise had taken the plastic Jesus in exchange for Minnie, Jakubiak told me.

When I got back to their flat, Martin and Louise were watching TV. I turned it off like I owned the place.

"Where's your baby?" I said. Martin chewed on his tongue and stared at my hands. I put them in my pockets. "Don't you realize how lucky you are?" I shouted. "Martin, look at me. What have you done?"

"We gave her to the church."

"Martin, you abandoned your baby."

"We got a new one," he said. "He's in the crib."

"You dumb bastard."

Martin just stared at me. "Boys are good babies," he said.

I picked up the baby Jesus. They had dressed it in a blue sleeper.

"His name is Mr. Wizard," Martin said. He turned the TV back on.

Jakubiak arranged for me to stop by the welfare office the morning the state people came for Minnie so I could say goodbye. Minnie was now a temporary ward of the state, and though I agreed with Jakubiak that that was the best thing, still I would miss her. She'd grow up in a real house now, with two average parents, people like Donna and I might have been.

I sat in Jakubiak's swivel chair, behind his cluttered desk, in a cramped cubicle. I jiggled Minnie in my right arm, teased her with a pacifier. I think I wanted her to cry. "She's smiling."

"You're a natural," Jakubiak said.

"Think so?" I held Minnie up, tickled her with my head. She made noises. "What do you say to a two-month-old?"

Jakubiak shrugged and smiled. "She's a cutie."

"Do you have any kids, Jakubiak?"

"Two. Boys."

"That's great."

The phone rang, Jakubiak answered it, said, "Right away," and hung up. "I'll take her down now, Robert, if that's okay?" he said.

"Yes." I told her goodbye, kissed her on the nose. "Jakubiak, let's have lunch."

"Sure."

I handed her over. "Alice and the Hat? Noonish?"

"I'll be there."

"One more kiss," I said.

After seeing Minnie, I drove around with the off-duty light on for a while, and found myself on Grafton Street in front of the house that Donna grew up in. I remembered when I was sixteen and had a crush on her how I would walk past this house seven times a day hoping she'd be on her porch, at a window, or out in the yard and she would see me and call to me. When that happened, we'd sit on the stoop and tell each other how we longed to live in Europe, Australia, Asia, anywhere but here, how neither of us would ever work nine-to-five, and all of that. Someone had put up vinyl siding over the shingles and paved the side yard. I drove away. Jakubiak had said that Minnie would be placed in a good home within the month, no problem. And nothing would happen to Martin and Louise except that they'd have to return Mr. Wizard. Eventually, Martin would get a vasectomy.

I pulled up to the diner, parked. I thought about Donna.

She'd gotten over me as surely as she got over Barry and Chris and music and herbs. She used to say I had no imagination or else I'd get on with my life; now I knew what she meant. It was ten before noon. I figured I'd call her tonight. I watched my eyes in the rearview mirror and rehearsed: Donna, it's Robert. Listen, you were right all along. I'm glad you're going through with the divorce. It's time I got on with my life. There's silence on the line. Donna? She says, Hello, Robert, and then maybe she says it's sad, isn't it, here at the end of everything. Or maybe she doesn't.

Shortly after noon, Jakubiak walked into the diner and joined me at my booth. He took off his gloves, hung up his coat, sat down, and rubbed his hands. He ordered a coffee. We sat and I told Jakubiak about the water and the stone.

MUST I BE CARRIED TO THE SKY ON FLOWERED BEDS OF EASE?

THIS MORNING EARLY I lugged the old sofa bed in from the back porch, dragged it to the kitchen, and fit it into the corner by the TV. I got the cushions and bolsters cleaned up as best I could and found some flannel sheets in the chifforobe.

My older boy came home today after fifteen years. He's come home to die. All my life I've had this trouble holding on to what loves me, and now here's Russell coming back, lifting me up with his ravaged body.

I'm fifty-seven years old and have always lived on these nineteen acres of cotton land. I've got the one boy that's wild, the other that's tame. I put Bobby through four years at LSU, and now he's with the post office and don't even call but for Christmas. Ain't been up to see me since his momma run off, and that's six years now. Russell, he's thirty-one, but has yet to find his niche. He's a drifter. Before today, the last I'd actually seen of Russell he was sixteen. He drove past me on the farm road, blowing dust up my lungs, in Johnny Carl Lamkin's Dodge coupe, which, come to learn, he'd stolen from behind Spats's Pharmacy and which was found two days later off the road in Breaux Bridge.

Russell did fourteen months in a Florida jail for holding up a 7-Eleven. Since then he keeps moving. Russell will once in a while call collect when he is drunk enough to talk. Sometimes he'll say, Daddy, do you remember this time or that. Like about the day when he was ten and told me he wasn't going to the cemetery with the family like we always did on Decoration Day. I said he was too.

"Won't."

"You'll do what I tell you. Get in the truck."

"No. Them uncles don't mean nothing to me."

I slapped him.

He smiled. "You can hit me all day, but you can't make me go." And I knew he was right. And now we might laugh about it when he phones. Usually, though, we have little to say to each other.

I was married to the boys' momma twenty-seven years, more out of habit, it turns out, than anything worth talking about. Funny thing is, I thought I loved her all that time, thought so right up until she showed me otherwise— she walked out, and I did not go after her. This was the day Bobby called from Baton Rouge to say he was engaged. Hazel cried at the news, and knowing I could not tolerate tears, walked out back to the junk pile. I stood on the porch watching, thinking I might say something, I didn't know what. She stared through the brambles and kudzu at Bobby's rusted tricycle. I called to her. She spoke to the pile like it was me. She said, "The boys are gone. What do we do now, Jesse?" It's then I realized that for twenty-seven years she'd had the one boy or both to care for, and we had never spoken about our future. The way I saw the future, it was just more of the present—more planting, chopping, harvesting, more sleeping at night, dinners, suppers, more watching the TV. She asked how much I loved her. I said, "Enough." She said she needed more than that. I said, "What do you need?" She said if I loved her, I'd know. She said, "Being alone is hard, Jesse, but not so hard as being alone with you." That's what she said. Then she left.

I drove her to the bus station in Monroe. We were quiet. I did not ask her to stay, it not being my way to force a person against her will. She told me she was going to her sister's in Ferriday. Hazel wore that red dress with black buttons and these new black shoes. I waited until she boarded the bus—she sat right up front by a window—and then I drove home.

Family has come and gone. Now I'm settled in simple seclusion, abandoned, so to speak, through my own doing. What it was rendered me solitary began the morning my daddy woke me, saying the baby had died in the night and

that Momma was delirious with fever and pain. He was
going to town after Dr. Bryant, he said, and told me to
follow him out behind the house. Daddy handed me a
shovel and the damp business swaddled in a flour sack
and said to dig it deep so the dogs don't get to it. I buried
the bundle Daddy called Ezekiel beneath the chinaberry,
and tried to summon the grief or the guilt I knew I should
feel. I pinched a thumbnail into my lip until it bled, but
all I felt was tired and far away. I tamped the soil with my
bare feet, drew my name in the dirt with my pointing fin-
ger, and then smoothed away the "Jesse Halliwell." I lay
down on the warm, damp mound. Next thing I know,
Daddy's kicking my feet, saying, "Jesse, your brother's in
heaven by now." Daddy crossed himself, moved his lips
like he was praying. He stared up into the tree. "We never
got to know him. That's the worst part."

Momma never recovered. Dr. Bryant explained as to how
there was a situation in Momma's womb that caused her
to expel the child and then finished its work on her. The
afternoon she died, Daddy fetched me at school in the old
black pickup. We stopped at the Farmers and Merchants
Bank and then over to Benton Mulhearn, the undertak-
er's. Daddy had me wait in the truck. I sat and listened to
the engine tick and the seat creak and tried to picture
Momma's face. I tried to remember her smell, the smell
that warmed and hugged me like a blanket. I saw the cot-
ton wagons lined up at the gin on Texas Avenue. So life
goes on, I thought. No matter that you think it shouldn't.
Daddy opened the door, hauled himself up in the seat,
and looked at me. "Wipe your eyes, boy," he said. "Too
late for that now." He let out the handbrake, cranked the

engine. It whined, stalled. "We got no more family, Jesse. Let it slip through our fingers."

What I knew even before Momma died was that Daddy had vanished into his love for her, was unable to reckon himself as a separate person. One evening I got up from bed to visit the outhouse and caught him kneeling on the kitchen floor, crying into Momma's lap, onto the hem of her apron. "You mustn't think you're a bad boy," she consoled him. I was so alarmed at the mystery of whatever dark secret drove him to his knees that I crept back to my room.

Daddy lost himself in religion, decided not to believe in disease, preferring sin as an explanation for death and other depravities, because sin is, I suppose, something you can prevent, at least. Shortly after Momma's funeral, he joined up with the Luna Church in Pine Grove and shut me out of his life except for the farming chores. He hired a Negro woman, Lottie Staples, to cook and tend to the house.

Then he brought home the Reverend Pettibone, who prayed over me in the parlor and cursed me when I would not pray with him. "Angel of Death" he called me. Said my soul was like the bayou, so black no light could enter. Light is love, he said. I considered the bayou and imagined snakes sliding through my spiritual parts. All this time, Daddy's kneeling in the doorway, his eyes cast to the floor as if there were shame in the room. Reverend Pettibone held my face in his hands and said, "Jesus loves you like your Momma done. Why do you drive Him away, too?"

Why I was unable to kneel with Daddy, or to seek solace in congregation, I cannot say. I suspected some connection between Daddy's head in Momma's lap and the death of Ezekiel and how that all led to the Luna Church, and I did not want to understand it. I would, I figured, be spared some painful knowledge through my ignorance. Reverend Pettibone said I'd only find peace in Jesus. I watched Daddy on his knees, his shoulders trembling just a little bit, his hands folded at his chest.

Without Momma, Daddy succumbed to the sin of constant recollection and grew weak with grief and sick with mourning. He got a slow-eating cancer when I was fourteen and suffered until I was nearly nineteen. The final year or so, he was confined to a sofa bed, nursed by Miss Lottie, the sofa bed against the back wall from where he could talk to the painting of the Nightly Savior over the kitchen stove, the Savior whose icy blue eyes followed me around the room. The last thing Daddy said was, "Jesse, where's your brother Ezekiel? He's got his chores to do." Miss Lottie cried. I said, "Ezekiel's in the field, Daddy." He shut his eyes and Miss Lottie sang "Flowered Beds of Ease." I walked out into the cotton, lay down, and listened to her.

Russell came home this afternoon, smaller than he was fifteen years ago. Told me he'd spent the last two months in a New Orleans hospital having all his blood removed and someone else's pumped in. Done that four different times. I picked him up at the Monroe airport. "Daddy," he said, "sometimes I can't even stand up. That's how it is." He carried everything he owned in a black nylon overnight bag. I helped Russell into the truck. Before I could scoot around to the driver's side and hop in, he was asleep, head against the window, mouth open. I watched him fight to catch a breath, the way he did when he was a baby. I heard a jet plane, listened to the pitch of its engines shift as it descended over the Interstate. I tried to remember Russell at sixteen. But it was like the only Russell I'd ever known was this one here nodding beside me, the one who had called me yesterday to ask if I would have him back.

In all those years he was gone, I never missed Russell. He was the red-haired boy who couldn't wait to leave, who drove out of my life before I got to know him. He had become a pleasant enough acquaintance, like a friend from school, who called once in a while to remind himself who he was. I thought about him, naturally, wondered some nights where he might be, but never with fondness or regret. That's what I told him yesterday when he asked could he come home. That's when he explained how he was dying. He told me how these purple bumps and blotches just came out on his legs one day and then blossomed like terrible flowers and petrified. "Just so you know what to expect," he said. He told me about medicines that left him feeling so adrift he didn't know where his hand left off and the spoon began, about good days when he'd be reckless enough to hope, and other days of fever and worse, and he told me about the plasma exchanges and how the doctors said, "No more."

After the call, I took a walk. I went looking for the weakness that would bring me strength. Here was Russell coming back to me who had done nothing to deserve this last chance to love my child. I walked across the brake, down through the poplars to where the old black pickup sits rusting on blocks. I yanked at the door. It creaked and rattled open. I ran my palm across the dusty, faded uphol-stery, looked over at the steering wheel, and saw those cotton wagons again and the Savior's icy blue eyes, that flour sack. I heard my daddy say, "The difference between me and you, Jesse, is you're whole. I'm only a piece of something else. I can't hold together without Ezekiel and your momma." And then I remembered the shame of death and felt the disgrace of having allowed this abomination to seize my boy.

Except for a chill, Russell said he felt much better when we reached home. I fixed up some beans and rice and we drank some bourbon at the kitchen table. Russell smiled, looked around the kitchen. "Nothing's changed," he said. "I'm glad."

"It's only been fifteen years."

"Seems longer. I should tell you where I've been."

"No need."

"Didn't think I'd ever come back. I wanted to almost as soon as I was gone. You know, all those times I called I was just waiting for you to tell me to come home." Russell shook his head. "I didn't know how to ask."

"I'm glad you're back, Russell."

"Feels good."

We were quiet, and then I said, "Does Bobby know?"

"No one knows but you."

"I think we'll get along, don't you, Russell?"

"I do."

"I used to bathe you in that sink."

"I remember. Every Saturday."

"Till you were four or five."

"I never thought I'd die this way, fading the way your daddy did," Russell said. "And not on my back in this here kitchen."

I said, "Russell, I got the TV there set up so you can see it without the window light shining on the screen."

Russell scratched his ear. He has such long, fine fingernails. "You know, Daddy, this won't be pretty. You could get some help."

"Don't need help."

When he fell asleep, I carried Russell to the sofa bed. He's as light and flimsy as a rattle-bag. I took his things off. Where his skin isn't blotched or rashed, it looks thick and doughy like if you pressed on it, your fingermarks would stay. I noticed how Russell smiled at the furniture. He said he's going to tell me about his life when we get the time. It's hard for me to think he ever left or ever was sixteen.

I'll have to call his mother. I haven't asked Russell why he did not go to her, and I won't. She'll want to visit. I can arrange to be out working. Haul off some of the junk pile to the brake and bury it. I'll call Hazel, tell her Russell's here, that he's asking for her.

Russell sleeps like a cat or a very old man, frequently, briefly, and soundly. He's woken three times tonight, damp with sweat, coughing. I watch, cool his brow when he starts. It must be nearly five, five-thirty. Looking out the window, I can just about see from here to the chinaberry. When its leaves get their green, I'll start fixing Russell's biscuits. He says there'll be days I have to feed him.

TO SAVE A LIFE

I'M FORTY-THREE years now without my husband, who died a young man in the war. I keep his photograph on the piano. Louis was a kind man and he made me laugh, but he'll always be thirty-three and will never understand what it's like to grow old, to watch your friends dry up with disease and your own body rebel. Louis smiles at me, Lucky Strike in the corner of his mouth, right leg propped up on the front bumper of our old Chevrolet. He even smiles when I get my Friday-afternoon migraine. At Union Station on the morning he left for the war, Louis held my head in his hands, kissed my eyes, and said, "No matter what happens, Eva, I'll always love you, and we'll always be together." Louis was wrong.

Eleven years ago I retired as a cafeteria worker for the Worcester School Department. I allow myself two weekly indulgences—a Wednesday wash and set and a Sunday-evening telephone call to my niece in San Diego. Well, actually, three indulgences—I play bingo Thursday nights at the church hall. At any rate, I live comfortably on my pension. But I needed to get out of the house, away from the TV and the vacuum cleaner, so I took a job two months ago at a fast-food place. I work the counter four mornings a week. Once in a while I'll do the drive-thru window.

I took my first paycheck to Zayre's and bought a pair of binoculars. They're made in Taiwan, have a German name, and cost me fifty-four dollars. Binoculars work the way memory does. They compress space the way memory compresses time. You're looking out over a long distance, and yet everything seems close, and all the important images are in focus. Right now I can close my eyes and see the frail red-haired doctor with tin glasses and pro-truding ears telling me I wouldn't have children; the Western Union boy with the rolled-up right pant leg, pushing his rattling bicycle up the walk, bearing a mes-sage from the War Department; Louis in a white tuxedo; my father, hatless, in a flannel shirt, carrying his black lunch box under his arm and throwing kisses as he walks up Pilgrim Avenue from the trolley stop. I can open my eyes, look through the binoculars out my window, and see the blue jay on the cement birdbath, a few spindly tomato plants clinging to bent stakes, a man on his piazza staring at the backs of hands, and beyond the roof of the house, the white spire of St. Anthony's Church. With binoculars you see the details, and they make all the difference. You see the half-dozen or so liver spots on the back of the man's hands, say, or the scar on his ring finger that runs from knuckle to knuckle below the gold wedding band. It's this ring, these spots, you realize, that are vital, not the flesh, but the scars on the flesh that change *a man* to *this man.*

Once when he tried to explain the war to me, Louis said, "Eva, you got to see the big picture." He talked about "freedom, honor, courage" and said the Allies were saving the world from evil. I nodded, but didn't understand. He sounded like a priest and I was never very clever with ideas. I did finally learn the meaning of the war that Easter morning in 1944 when I walked into our bedroom, opened a bureau drawer, and smelled the trace of my dead husband on his clothes.

I bought the binoculars to spy on Raymond. I've known Raymond longer than I've known anyone, and all that time we've been neighbors. Of course, the neighborhood's changed in those forty-six years. It looks the same, the rows of shingled bungalows, the small, neat lawns out front, and the maple trees. But it feels different. You don't see neighbors out horsing around on a summer night like you used to. People here stay inside, keep quiet, drive cars. Anyway, I'm trying to save Raymond's life whether he likes it or not, and to do that I have to watch for signs.

For the first time in his life, Raymond feels all alone in the world. Being alone is terrifying. Some days you feel like a shell, not the kind that explodes, but the kind that fractures. You figure if you knock into anything or anyone, you'll crack, just like that. So you sit. And that's one way to survive, I suppose, but like I told Father Ducharme, a person has to do more than survive.

But these days Raymond just sits in that chaise longue on his piazza wearing that gray "Weirs Beach" sweatshirt and that ridiculous orange vinyl ballcap. I've been studying Raymond from my pantry window. With the binoculars, I can even read the decade-old fishing license pinned to the front of the cap. His eyes have iced over. He's become inaccessible, even to me, even to his son, the playboy attorney from Fitchburg.

Raymond Lucier is a retired housepainter, veteran, and widower. The day my Louis and I moved into this house, Raymond walked over with three bottles of beer in his hand, introduced himself, and helped Louis unload the upright piano from the pickup we'd borrowed from my East Brookfield cousins.

Father Ducharme, our pastor at St. Anthony's, says I can best help Raymond by praying, of course, by stopping in for chats, baking him bread, friendly, neighborly things like that, which I do. But what I really want to do some days is grab his bony little shoulders and give him a healthy shake, holler in his good ear, tip him off the chaise longue, and tell him the moles are killing his tomato plants. Raymond doesn't even tend his garden anymore.

In the spring of 1932, Raymond married Ruthie Levasseur, the only girl he'd ever dated. The two families lived in the same triple-decker on Grafton Street, and as Raymond tells it, his courtship of Ruthie began in a sandbox. Then last year, after fifty-five years of marriage, on a Sun-

day night in November, Ruthie dried the super dishes, took
her *Family Circle* from the magazine rack in the den, kissed
Raymond on the forehead, and went upstairs to read. Ray-
mond found her slumped on the floor against the bath-
room door.

I think it's so much sadder when the wife goes first. A
husband's never had to make sense of Venetian blinds and
traverse rods or sideboards and radiators; never had to
combine all these puzzling fixtures and pieces into a home.
Raymond found Ruthie's clothespin bag hung from a nail
at the top of the cellar stairs, and he started to cry. He
couldn't understand why she would make a clothespin bag
from his old flannel workshirt. "We had the money to buy
a new one," he said.

In the two months after Ruthie's death, Raymond would
call a couple of times a week and ask where the canned
carrots were, and I'd tell him, "Second cabinet from the
wall, third shelf, behind the waxed beans." He'd call back
in twenty minutes. "Where's the can opener?" I'd say,
"Come over for supper, Raymond. I've got more pot roast
than I could eat in a week." As we ate, I'd say, "Raymond,
we all miss you at bingo," or "Raymond, Armand Goulet
was wondering if you were still planning to help with the
parish picnic this year." Anything to draw him out, get
him talking and thinking about other people again. I was
worried. Three months after Ruthie's death, Raymond
almost never left his house. He had relinquished all of his
enthusiasms. He was seventy-four then, but acted like he
was ninety-five. However as Father Ducharme pointed out,
Raymond still went to ten-fifteen Mass every Sunday. We
grasped at that as a hopeful sign.

In early February, Raymond began finding these obscure
items around the house. First, he noticed a nylon stocking
wrapped tightly around the trap plug in the kitchen sink
drain. Then he discovered a matchbook, folded twice and
wedged beneath the leg of an end table. He brought the
stocking and the matchbook to my house along with a
yardstick that had a dust rag tied to its end. He placed
them all on my kitchen table and asked me to examine
them. The stocking was seamless and damp; the match-
book advertised stamps from around the world; the yard-
stick had inches on one side, centimeters on the other, and
came compliments of Spag's Hardware. Raymond smiled
for the first time since his wife had died. He explained that
none of these items had been in the house when Ruthie
was alive, and so they could very well be messages from
her. Did I know what they could mean? "It's possible they
don't mean a thing, Raymond," I said.

Raymond resumed his investigation unfazed by my
skepticism. Behind the Maytag in the cellar, he found a
box of Marlboros and a mayonnaise-jar lid used as an
ashtray containing three clinched butts, lipstick on each
filter. Ruthie didn't smoke when she was alive, he informed
me. I told Raymond she did so smoke only she was afraid
to do it in front of him. He didn't believe me. For the next
week, Raymond presented me with the articles he'd
unearthed in his house. He kept them all in what I
recognized as Ruthie's shopping tote, the one with "Le
Bag" in large blue letters on the side. He had a pic-
kle jar crammed with assorted buttons, a skeleton key, a
block of gray wood, three soft eyeglass cases, a photo
of a small one-eyed dog wearing a party hat, a roll of

faded flock wallpaper, and more. The treasure increased daily.

I said to him, "Now, Raymond, don't you think all of these things might have been in the house all along, but you simply failed to notice them?" He smiled for the second time since Ruthie's death. "That's what you'd like me to think," he said.

Raymond stopped his visits. I had failed him as a judge. He no longer arrived with his evidence, but his archaeology continued. From my kitchen window I'd see him on the piazza examining his artifacts. I watched him inspect a skeleton key. He smelled it and then held it to his ear as if it were whispering to him. That's when I said a special little prayer to Ruthie herself. "Ruthie," I said, "if you really are sending messages to this man, why don't you just come right out with it. This detective business isn't dignified."

And then for three days Raymond failed to appear on his piazza. When you're our age and live alone, you learn to check in with people on a regular basis. You buy your paper at Monahan's Pharmacy every morning; you visit the Mechanics Bank on Friday, Weintraub's deli on Saturday, that sort of thing. It's a simple system that will alert people should something happen. Raymond was sending me an alarm even if he was unaware of it.

He didn't answer the phone. I hung up and headed across the backyard. I tapped through a thin sheet of ice on the birdbath and realized I was in no hurry to reach Raymond's. When I did, the back door was unlocked, and I walked in. Raymond stood shirtless and silent in the middle of his kitchen. He was powdered from hair to shoes in white plaster dust like he'd been dampened and dredged in flour. Only his narrow eyes and the pry bar in his right hand were black. The knuckles were scraped raw. He wasn't wearing dentures, and his cheeks had caved in.

"Where are your teeth, Raymond?"

"I lost them."

"What on earth are you doing?"

"Looking for Ruthie."

Raymond had chipped the parlor fireplace apart brick by brick, pried the casings off the first-floor windows, opened deep gashes in the four kitchen walls, ripped the treads from the risers on the staircase, stripped the lino-leum from the pantry floor, and most recently, it seemed, torn down the hallway ceiling.

"Just look at yourself, Raymond." I called Father Ducharme, who called an ambulance. I wanted to cry.

I remember a night when I was six. My father came home from work at the wire mill, kissed Mother and me, pulled off his boots, draped his woolen socks over the radiator, and poured himself a beer from a jug in the ice-box. I waited for him to take the green pack of cigarettes from his trousers pocket, sit on the rocker, and motion for me to climb up into his lap. I did. I leaned in against his chest. He squeezed my dimpled knee. He smelled like burning leaves. My father kept his life simple and unclut-tered, without the worries rich people have. All he needed was his family, our warm kitchen, cold beer, and a job to go to in the morning. Money wouldn't make him a better wire cutter or me a concert pianist, he said, and since it couldn't even make pea soup taste better, what good was it then?

"For one thing, Giles Paradis," Mother said, "we could go dancing at the Frohshin Club once in a while."

My father tugged at my braids. "Are you giving your mother these fancy ideas?" he asked me. "'Cause if you are I'll just have to tickle you to death."

"Not me," I said.

"Anyway, who needs a ballroom when we have a kitchen?" My father set me down, stood, hugged Mother, whirled and waltzed her around the kitchen, all the time whistling "And the Band Played On" while I applauded from the rocker and Mother laughed herself to tears.

I try to remember him that way, barefoot and innocent. He lost his job and the sense of meaning he had manufactured for his life in the Depression. He grew bitter and morose. We left our flat and moved in with my grandparents. I quit secretarial school to take in laundry with Mother. Life for the poor turned out to be more complicated than my father had wished. The family alone, he discovered, was not enough to hold his life together. At first, perhaps, he thought he had lost control, but then shivered to realize that he'd never had any. That's what I think. No job now. No fault of his own. Nothing to be done around the house that we hadn't done. At first, he'd leave early in the morning, stay out of Mother's hair until supper time, and then he took to staying out later with friends. My father was thirty-seven when he left us to wander off to Montana, where he'd heard they were looking for men to build a dam.

I wonder how Maurice Lucier will remember his father.

Maurice, as I said earlier, is Raymond's fancy son. He has four cars, three homes, and two ex-wives. When I spoke with Maurice at his mother's wake, he told me about the twenty-foot cabin cruiser he'd just bought. I said, "What are you going to do with a cabin cruiser in Fitchburg?" Maurice was tanned, vigorous, and practical. He told me he didn't have time to worry.

When we sent Raymond off to the hospital, I called Maurice and told his answering machine what had happened. The following morning Maurice drove to Worcester in his charcoal-gray German car with "Lucier" plates and surveyed the damage done at Raymond's. He scribbled notes in a small book and said he'd have his men take care of the repairs. He used Raymond's phone to call the hospital and an insurance company.

Maurice thanked me for getting his father to the hospital. "God only knows what he would have done to this place if you hadn't arrived." He shook his head. "I guess he just snapped."

At my new job, I see them every day, the senior citizens who tramp in for their biscuits and coffees, occasionally nodding to the other regulars. They come up for their refills. They dawdle here, having no place to go but home. They're caught in the past is why, always considering their lives, not living them. "He was a peach of a husband," they tell me. "We had a good life." Memory that should cleanse like the small rain drowns them in its flood. Sentimentality is killing them. I told Raymond in the hospital, "There's nothing in your past so valuable it should bankrupt your future." I may be hardhearted like my niece says, but that's what I believe.

A person has to do more than survive. Endurance is the easy part. A person has to overcome the loss of father, husband, friend, unborn child. I loved my Louis dearly, but he left me. They all leave. Sometimes I think I go on just to show them I can live without them. Father Ducharme says what makes life so precious is the joy we earn by accepting the Lord as our Savior. That may be, but what makes life holy is our knowledge of the absolute sadness at the heart of our existence. We are, each of us, alone in the darkness.

Raymond spent seven weeks in the hospital. The doctors said it was acute depression, not Alzheimer's. They said he had no recollection of demolishing his house, but was able to talk about his wife's death, something they considered a healthy sign. They sent him home with his son's qualified consent and several vials of pills.

Maurice called and asked if I would look in on Raymond periodically. I'll do more than that, I assured him. I had just come home from Zayre's with the binoculars. Maurice asked if I thought Raymond might be better off getting married again. I said what on earth for. He said that way he'd be taken care of. Only a man would think of that, I said.

"If this sort of thing happens again, Eva, I'm afraid I'll have to put him in a nursing home. What else can I do?"

"He's your father," I said. "You could move him into your house."

"That wouldn't be feasible, Eva, and you know it."

I began stopping by Raymond's on my way home from

work with a bag of burgers and fries. Raymond was grateful for the lunches even though he had some trouble chewing with the new teeth. He told me he was taking his pills, and although they calmed him down, they left him without the energy to socialize. I said that would come with time.

"Why is my son calling every few days?" he asked.

"He's concerned about you."

"He never used to call."

"You know he's a busy man, the biggest lawyer in Fitchburg."

"So why does he bother me with these phone calls?"

"He's worried. You've been sick, Raymond."

"I have?"

"Raymond, listen to me. Except in your head, Ruthie is dead."

With my encouragement and a shoebox full of seed packets from Maurice, Raymond planted a garden and promised me all the plum tomatoes I could can. Over the Memorial Day weekend, he went boating with Maurice and Maurice's secretary on Lake Winnipesaukee and came back with a pink face and a gray sweatshirt. It was his first time on a boat since the war, he said, but he hadn't lost his sea legs. And then we laughed about the day in 1942 when he and my Louis walked downtown to the recruiting station and joined the navy because they liked the uniforms. Not until they got home that night did they remember that neither of them could swim.

But if Raymond was improving, it seemed to me that he

was doing so grudgingly. His new teeth bothered him. Sores developed on his gums, he said, so he stopped wearing the upper plate and began eating baby food. After Mass on Sundays he smiled at the people who greeted him, but then would ask me who that was, the one with the hearing aid and white mustache. I'd say, you know Armand Goulet; you two went to grammar school together. "Goulet?" he'd say.

I told Father Ducharme I was worried Raymond might still be crazy and that maybe we should do something. He said perhaps "crazy" was not the word to use in this case. He suggested "senile." Well, not only was he senile then, but he seemed to be embracing this dotage like a wife. Which brings us to last Friday night.

I know why I get my headaches on Friday afternoons at three, but there's nothing I can do to stop them. I've seen the doctors, taken their pills. On Good Friday 1944, I received a telegram from the War Department telling me that my Louis's ship had been sunk off the Marshall Islands and there were no survivors. The migraine starts with a tickle in my right ear. When the nausea begins, I go to bed, lie on my left side, and wait for the pain to rock me to sleep. When I wake up at eleven-thirty, I feel refreshed.

When I woke last Friday, rain clattered on the metal drainpipe outside my window. This was, I feared, one of those signs I had been watching for. I put on my robe and got my umbrella. Raymond was in his garden, kneeling in the mud with a long two-pronged fork. He told me he was weeding the tomatoes. I took him aside, dried his hair with a dish towel, and got him into some dry pajamas. All the while Raymond sat quietly like a chastised child. "Raymond, you shouldn't be gardening in the rain, not at midnight." I took him to his bed, fed him one of his white pills, and tucked him in.

Raymond smiled at me. "Good night, Ruthie," he said.

"Raymond," I said, "you can't go on in this miserable way."

I didn't want to surrender Raymond to a nursing home—too many rocking chairs, too little hope. A nursing home would simply indulge Raymond's senility with understanding or ignore it with medication. So I didn't call Maurice. Instead, I took Raymond for a walk around the neighborhood the next morning. Raymond had filled himself so full of his dead wife that there was no longer room in his life for Armand Goulet or any of his other friends, not even me, just Ruthie. Ruthie without scars or liver spots, a Saint Ruthie so great and holy that everything else was remembered through the wrong end of the binoculars. The purpose of this walk last Saturday was to focus his memory, I hoped.

We stopped at the drive-thru bank across from St. Anthony's. I reminded Raymond that this had been Tagman's Bakery until twenty years ago. We always stopped there after Mass for bulkies and then we'd go next door to Whitman's for our cream cheese. He remembered. And he remembered Arsenault's butcher shop three blocks down on Green Street. He asked me where the stores had gone.

"No place. They just closed."

He shook his head. "No more trolleys either."

"No more trolleys."

"What happened to the Franco-American Club?"

"Blew down in the '38 hurricane, remember?"

"We had our reception there, Ruthie and I."

"It's just apartment buildings now."

Raymond raised his arms and stood like Father Ducharme does at the end of Mass when he says, "Go in peace."

"I don't want any of this," Raymond said, and I knew he meant more than just the neighborhood. "I miss my wife."

"She's dead, Raymond."

He looked at me. "Don't you ever want Louis back?"

"Louis is gone," I said. "You're all I have." And I thought, did I hear myself right? All I have is Raymond?

That's when it struck me. I needed Raymond. There's nobody left I care about in quite the same way, nobody I've known for forty-six years, nobody else who remembers my Louis. If Raymond dies, nobody on earth will remember that Eva Paquette was once loved by an exhilarating young man, a tender and handsome man who wanted to stay with her forever. Raymond is my last witness.

Raymond is sitting on his piazza and staring at the liver spots on the backs of his hands. I'm at the kitchen window with my binoculars, focusing on those hands, and I see him turn and turn his wedding band. I'll save Raymond whether he likes it or not, I tell myself. I'll convince him that he owes something to the living, that the dead are snug in Father Ducharme's heaven, flush with happiness and beatific vision. We're all we have, Raymond, you and me, I'll say.

I could help him. Have him tell me the story of how he got the scar the night he and Louis got drunk after learning they were being separated. Louis was finally going to see some action; Raymond was stuck stateside. I could even tell him I'm Ruthie. That's what he called me Friday night. I have her white hair, dark eyes, glasses. I could put on Ruthie's green housedress; he'd never know.

Look at him over there chattering away. I wish I could tell you he's talking to himself, but he's talking with Ruthie about the cigarettes behind the Maytag. He's laughing. Louis used to do that. Sometimes I'd catch him talking to his tools out in the garage, telling the chisel how to finesse an angle on the wood or something. I used to laugh, and he'd say don't spy on me like that, Eva. And then he'd hug me. Louis and Raymond, two of a kind.

When I put down the binoculars, all I can see is a thin man sitting by himself. He could be almost anyone. And if I don't look close, then I can fill in the features.

A week after I learned of Louis's death, I received his month-old letter. The envelope was soiled, folded, and taped. Enclosed was a brief note and a two-by-one-inch photograph. "Dear Eva," Louis wrote, "I've made some friends who'll be yours, too, when this war is over. My first night home I'll rent a white tuxedo and we'll go dancing. I miss you always. Love, Louis." His P.S. directed me to the creased photo of him and Raymond taken days before Louis shipped out. The stark contrast of the tiny picture blurred all of the details. Two sailors posed in front of a gunmount. I stare at the hands, the smiles, and pretty soon I can't tell which one is Louis.

WHAT
FOLLOWS IN THE
WAKE OF LOVE

Belle Glade, Florida, 1955

Three of our colored boys found parts of Gonzalla Haz-
ard out in the slash pines, out there behind the Farm Labor
Supply Center. Only way they knew it was Gonzalla was
this tattoo of a crown of thorns on his left arm. "This kind
of murder ain't normal," they said. "Something devilish
going on." Gonzalla's woman said to me, "Sheriff, what's
Gonzalla's babies going to do now?"

I know Gonzalla's got these two uncles living with him

for the season, new boys to the county, from up around
Indian River somewhere. Only got nine fingers and three
eyes between them. I make it my business to talk to them
first, and I find out right off that Gonzalla was over in
Pahokee last Friday night at the Shuffle-Inn. Shuffle-Inn's
this juke joint famous for troubles. Holy Rollers from the
South Bay Pentecostal always trying to pray it out of exis-
tence, even worked some kind of hoodoo on it one time. I
said, "You all with Gonzalla, Uncles?" thinking to myself
that maybe I'm looking at the perpetrators right here on
this rickety front porch. "Sure we was," they told me, "only
we be asleep behind the produce mart by midnight."

I sent my deputy, Elvis Redwine's boy, up to Pahokee
to ask some questions. What Kyle finds out is that Gon-
zalla and this little baby doll drank three, maybe four, bot-
tles of Jax together and then checked into the Flamingo
Motel out round back by the old depot. Kyle spoke with
the Reverend Wamul Owens, who testified that he saw
them, both of them, Gonzalla and that harlot, strut into
the motel all tricked out like hot little circus monkeys, he
said. Saw three people leave. That's right, the Reverend
said, three: Gonzalla, the woman, and some big old Indian
boy. And they was all three drinking beers.

Meanwhile, I get a call from Mr. Wardell Heflin, who
wonders if it might not be wise to lock the workers inside
the Center until the crime is solved, or at least until his
crop is in. We've been down this road before, Mr. Heflin
and I. Sure, I could lock them up. For their own protec-
tion, I could say. Could do it easy. Find plenty of old boys
around here like nothing better than swaggering around

in the dark with rifles and dogs earning themselves some county money. But I won't do it 'cause I don't think it's right.

Course, if I don't find the boy that done this killing, or the woman at least, I'm afraid we're going to have us some trouble. You know what the uncles told me? Told me they heard the pickers over to Cedell's Barbecue talking about signing off in the morning and driving over to Clewiston to work the cane fields. I said, "Uncles, you keep this news to yourselves."

Just the idea of all these beans rotting in his fields makes Mr. Heflin mad. He kind of thinks this county belongs to him, and if he hears talk of migrants moving off before the harvest ends, I'll probably have to deal with those nasty fools he calls field bosses again. Intimidation is against the law, I've told him. Might as well talk to a cypress knee, though, as talk to a rich man about freedoms. Mr. Heflin, he'll pass his tongue along his upper teeth and suck on that ivory toothpick of his. He'll give me that look. And then you just know my ulcer's going to kick up again. Be drinking milk and cream till I spit. Course the wife sees me on milk and she starts. She frets and sulks and calls the preacher's wife and then the preacher himself shows up for dinner one Sunday. She'll end up crying like she does, heaving her shoulders on the bed, making things worse. She'll leave me a note at the breakfast table. It will say, "Henry, I don't care about no new Studebaker. What am I going to do if you're dying in the hospital?"

"You ought to be searching those cabins along the lake, Henry," Mr. Heflin tells me. I'm standing at the foot of his front stairs leaning up on the balls of my boots. "Come

and sit, Henry." Mr. Heflin motions me to the smaller of
two wicker chairs on the veranda. We sit. Mr. Helfin's wife,
Terlina, lives in an iron lung on the second floor—polio.
Mr. Heflin keeps a young thing not so discreetly secured
at the Deleon Hotel in town. He goes on, "Her name's
Lavonda Rose."

"Who's that, Mr. Heflin?"

"The harlot at the motel. In Pahokee. With Hazard."
He proceeds to tell me that this Lavonda and her male
cohort must have driven back to Belle Glade with Gon-
zalla, forced him down a farm road, and murdered him.

"Why do you suppose they chopped him to pieces, Mr.
Heflin?"

"Is that important, Henry? Now see here," he says to
me, "I've done your investigating for you. Now it is up to
you to bring these criminals swiftly to justice."

"Mr. Heflin, if you don't mind my asking, how did you
come by all this information?" I said but knew, of course,
that money is more persuasive than justice.

"I want my workers back in the fields, Henry. I'm mak-
ing it your job to see that they are on that truck in the
morning."

Mr. Helfin's man, Julius, appeared on the veranda with
a silver tray on which he balanced two tumblers of bour-
bon and a small black revolver, the drinks for each of us,
the pistol for Mr. Heflin. We thanked him.

"Mr. Heflin, you can't force colored people to do what
they don't want to do, not anymore you can't."

"You amuse me, Henry." Mr. Heflin sipped his bour-
bon.

"Seems to me you want things the way they used to be

before the war." And now I sipped. "'It ain't ever going to be like that again, Mr. Heflin. I'm sorry for you and your kind, but it just ain't.'"

Mr. Heflin drew the pistol from his lap and cocked the trigger. "Perhaps you're right, Henry." He aimed and fired at the green anole sunning itself on the banister. It disappeared in a burst of splinters. "In the past, I suppose, I would not even have bothered myself with the death of a nigger." He replaced the pistol on the silver tray, nodded to Julius, and stood. "Give my best to your lovely wife, Henry."

I figure I owe it to the wife—the Studebaker, I mean. Carlene ain't been real well since her only child died the way he did. Donald was hers from the marriage with the musician. Made it all the way through Korea without a scratch, Donald did, comes home, mopes and pouts about the house, falls in with a shiftless crowd, and winds up impaled by a forklift at the packing plant in Loxahatchee. Pinned to the wall like a butterfly.

I met Carlene while investigating the homicide. Suddenly, she needed someone to care for, and I was just as happy to get out of my trailer and into something more comfortable. But anyway, because she's a Baptist or something, or maybe because her family's related to the Wallaces of Boynton Beach, if that means anything to you, or for some other reason I can't fathom, Carlene absolutely refuses to ride in my cruiser. She says she feels common in it. I tell her we are common. Trashy, then, she says. So I thought I'd buy us a car for our fourth anniversary. Nothing new, naturally, but recent like that '52 Studebaker coupe out at Tommy Kincaid's World of Cars. That way we'd have more time with each other and I could get her out of that house awhile. Maybe someday take a proper vacation. I've been to Tallahassee myself, to a sheriffs' convention, and I think Carlene would like it there, the air-conditioned movie houses, smartly dressed people in restaurant windows, and all the work that goes on so cleanly inside of buildings.

Kyle and I found Lavonda and her boyfriend out at Blondin's Fish Camp having themselves a regular honeymoon. They were tucked away in Cabin 14, windows closed, shades drawn, door locked. In a clearing to the side of the cabin sat these three filthy children, two of them chewing dirt, the eldest, a girl about seven maybe, scratching the ears of a spindly old hound. All four were silent. Gonzalla's Chevrolet stood in the scattered shade of a pine. Kyle tugged the floral drapery off the front seat, and we saw where blood had blackened the fabric. I took another magnesia pill and nodded to Kyle. The dog whimpered and the children stood. Kyle fired a round into the lock on the cabin door.

You either hate this swamp and you leave it, or you hate it and you remain. Some, like Mr. Heflin, stay on to wrest whatever they can salvage from the imposition of their wills on the land and the people. Most others stay because they can't leave. Too poor, maybe, or too limited. That was Mam's word for folks around Belle Glade. Mam left. Got tired of bleaching mildew from the kitchen walls, tired of cotton dresses clinging to her damp skin, tired of water-bugs in the larder and moccasins in the outhouse. "To live here, you got to breathe water, is all," Daddy would joke with Mam when she complained. Remember now, there were no ceiling fans then, nothing to cool the steam of summer air, and no canals or drainage ditches, no farms even, and no dikes holding back the lake. Life was surely more uncertain and uncomfortable.

This one night we're all sitting on the porch. Mam's rocking, slapping at mosquitoes as loud as she can. Dad-dy's telling me a story about how the glades were all under the ocean until this Indian god rose it up so his people wouldn't drown. Mam stopped her rocking. "Didn't raise it high enough," she says. "Decent folks ought not to live like this, Lester, like amphibians—never clean, never even dry, never safe or rested, always having to move to keep ahead of the predators 'cause nothing that stops can sur-vive out here. I swear," she says, "even the damn grass has teeth."

Whenever Mam mentioned saw grass, that was my cue to fetch her bottle of Dr. Rowland's System Builder and her jam jar—"because ladies do not slurp from tea-spoons," was Mam's explanation. Daddy, he's quiet like he gets until Mam, having swallowed her medicine, says that the Devil himself can take this land. Daddy's in the dark across the porch. I can't see him but I know he's making tiny circles with his finger on his bald spot. Daddy says, "At least it's our land." That was his answer for everything.

What we owned, and this was before Daddy lost it to a

bank in the Depression, was half an acre, and you wouldn't call it land exactly, just a piece of this one vast, trembling mat sliding south from Okeechobee to the Keys. Centuries of rotted vegetation being sucked into the black muck. I used to think it was alive—the earth I mean, the way the Indians did—from the noises it made and the smells it leaked. Made me think it was jealous of anything rising above it. Least, that's what I thought as a child.

Mam asked could I bring my geography book home from school. I often did, and after supper me and her would sit at the table with a lamp and search through the pictures. One night Mam decided that Tennessee must be the roof of the country the way on page 95 the snow lay so thick and comforting in the Smokies. She told me there were reindeer in Tennessee, reindeer and penguins, even though that fact was not mentioned in the book. That comes in high school geography, she assured me. Reindeer, penguins, and log cabins with all their cracks chinked up with moss. Log cabins with fireplaces and electricity and indoor toilets. Mam said her sister, Elizabeth, the private secretary, lived in Gatlinburg and that we, meaning Mam and me, had been invited to visit her as soon as the school let out. Daddy said it's good you're going to see your sister and all, but the boy stays. I need him here.

For a while there were postcards, which I read to Daddy. Color vistas of mountains and fog and pastel-leafed trees. And then pictures of unusual buildings—a dairy bar shaped like a milk can, a souvenir shop that looked like a teakettle, restaurants like tugboats, derbies and barrels of root beer. Mam sent one card of just a blue Greyhound coach.

A forward window was circled and arrowed. "My seat," she had printed. Daddy said, "She don't own it."

Then Mam wrote that some clever Yankee doctors had advised her not to return so quickly to the thick, damp, tubercular Florida air. Since she no longer wished to burden dear Elizabeth, she would travel instead to Chicago. She only hoped her lungs were not already beyond salvation. The next spring Mam wrote that she had landed a job at a boardinghouse frequented by commercial travelers. That's when Daddy told me. Took me, in fact, to the O-kee-doke Club, bought me my first beer, and me only eleven or twelve years old, and says, "Son, your mother never had no sister."

Now Carlene's case is like the opposite of Mam's. When her Donald was only six months old, Carlene's husband, a cornet player, went off to do a gig in West Palm and never came back. Never wired money. Nothing. What Carlene should have done is called those Wallaces in Boynton Beach to come and fetch her and her child. But she is a proud woman and would not allow herself to be seen in the harsh light of poverty and abandonment. And she could not write to her father, a circuit rider in south Georgia who had disowned her following her elopement. Preachers are often quick to disinherit and sluggish to forgive. Still, she had the house, and she stayed and raised her boy with the eventual help of her second husband, a junior-high football coach whose last wish as he lay dying of emphysema was that Donald join the army and defend his country.

So anyway, back at Blondin's Fish Camp the two of them, Lavonda Rose and her Indian, are lying on the floor oblivious in the middle of the one dark room when we come busting in. She's on her stomach, face covered by the damp blanket of her hair, wearing one of those Japanese kimono deals all the soldiers brought back from the war. Large scarlet-and-lemony flowers on her shoulders like she'd fallen into a garden. The man's on his back snoring, sweating and shirtless, with one leg draped across her butt, and when Kyle kicks him conscious, he's staring down the barrel of Kyle's shotgun. Across the room, the green dial of a radio glows and Hank Williams is singing a song about someone not loving someone like they used to, which is funny, you see, on account of Lavonda herself is null and void on narcotics and her boyfriend turns out to be a deaf-mute Seminole name of Andrew Jackson, so Hank's just pleading into the void until me and Kyle come along.

Andrew Jackson's from Big Cypress, we find out, and until last Friday wrestled alligators at a snake farm on 441 across in Hendry County. Seems Friday, Andrew was fired for killing a thirty-five-year-old fourteen-foot bull gator who'd been all along the farm's star attraction. Like falling from a barstool after that, I imagine. Falling all the way to this musty cabin on Okeechobee, passed out on a linoleum floor with a wilted hooker and her, or someone's, three children, and wanted for murder.

Andrew Jackson began sobbing and shook Lavonda's shoulder. Kyle said, "I wonder what she's dreaming about." Probably love, is what I thought. Kyle tapped his foot to the music and I had this crazy notion right then that this rendezvous here was in some way romantic—out here by the lake, away from the world, yourself and a woman, the radio's on, the drinks are like fire, you talk and love until you find some peace. With a car, I thought, Carlene and I could drive ourselves to some secluded bungalow just like this. We'll sit on the porch after dinner, quietly. I'll be looking down at the grassy shoreline, and I'll realize how the night's like the future, so quiet you don't hear it coming. Suddenly you can't see the lake any more. Put down that book a minute, Carlene, I'll say. She'll smile. You happy? I'll ask her. I said, "Kyle, shut down that radio."

"She be spawning now, Sheriff," the uncles tell me. Gonzalla's woman, Theola Dunn, writhing like an eel on a skillet, is giving birth to the last of Gonzalla's children on the floor of this tenant shack. I've come to tell her something about the murder. Uncles tell me I got to be the doctor. "Doctor catches the baby, that's what," they say. I kneel between the great brown thighs and immediately a smooth, leathery child slithers into my hands. I want to wipe the foam and blood from its face, but he's squeezing my wrist with his tiny hands, each with four padded digits. "That's for sure one of ours," the uncles say. "Just look at those webbed toes." I study this arrowheaded, horny-lipped thing and notice the feathery pink gills below the earholes. They must lose those when they're weaned. I wanted to see did it have a tail, but that's when the dream ended and I rolled out of bed so as not to wake Carlene, and dressed to meet Mr. Heflin's truck at the Center.

The field hands, some more hungover than usual, met the truck at dawn, and so did Mr. Heflin, pleased to see that his harvest would now be completed in an orderly fashion. He congratulated me in front of the workers for solving the murder so swiftly, which only he and I and his informer knew was not at all true. Meanwhile, Gonzalla's woman had found herself a new man and told me that the children weren't none of Gonzalla's nohow. He was just another mouth to feed, is all, she says. Sounded like the words of a woman scorned and still fatally in love. Her new man, a yellow-black from up north named Roosevelt Holmes, sent the uncles packing. Said them few gnarly fingers gave him the willies.

By the time the trial commenced, Gonzalla's little family, along with this Roosevelt and just about anyone else who might have had an interest in the fate of Gonzalla's killers, had vanished from Belle Glade—the workers to follow the harvest north to the Carolinas, Mr. Heflin to do whatever it is he does in Havana with his sweet young thing, and Gonzalla's accumulated remains to his mama up in Forrest City, Arkansas. The zealous Reverend Owens, however, became a fixture at our jail. He had appointed himself Lavonda's spiritual adviser. Every afternoon at one he came wearing his iridescent green suit and porkpie hat and wiping his brow with a white handkerchief.

Lavonda confessed and threw herself on the mercy of the court. Confessed that she and Gonzalla had been carrying on an intermittent harvest-time love affair for seven years and that one or possibly two of her children belonged to Gonzalla. Confessed that Andrew Jackson was a sexual powerhouse whose carnal nature and musky scent drove her to a frenzy. Confessed the grisly details of the night in question.

Lavonda had invited Gonzalla back to the room she shared with Andrew Jackson at the Flamingo. What then began, according to the prosecuting attorney, as a relatively innocent sexual diversion, a Gonzalla sandwich, so to speak, escalated into something bestial, unthinkable, and yes, gentlemen of the jury, fatal.

Lavonda confessed that Andrew Jackson just sort of snapped the night they did Gonzalla, probably because he lost his job, she figured, or maybe, like the Reverend says, he was into some kind of Satan worship like so many of those pagan Indians are. Something had made him furious, she just couldn't be certain what. He suddenly went at the little man, slicing him with a fish knife, and began to fillet him like a bullhead, while all the time Gonzalla's screaming for mercy and whatnot 'cause he's still alive, you see.

She knew it was wrong, what they done, but at the time, Judge, she said, at the time, to be quite honest—having placed her left hand on the Bible and sworn before her personal Lord and Savior, Jesus Christ, to tell the whole truth and nothing but—to be truthful, she was kind of excited by it all, by her strapping Seminole lover, the starry night, the Chevrolet, the money in Gonzalla's billfold, all these sudden changes in her life. Of course, now she was sincerely sorry that it all had to happen. You can see for yourself she's telling the truth, her lawyer says.

Lavonda was found guilty of prostitution, aiding and abetting a felon, etc., given a three-year suspended sentence so that she could see to her children, and ordered by Judge Lanny Purvis to attend weekly pastoral counseling sessions at Reverend Owens's Rose of Sharon Free Will Baptist Church.

Andrew Jackson was not so fortunate. Of course, he did not testify, since he could not, but he did affix his mark and his thumbprint to a confession drawn up by his own attorney. And he did act out his own slow-motion version of the murder right there in the courtroom with Kyle playing the part of Gonzalla. Andrew might see his next alligator around 1986, if there are any left by then. More than likely, however, he'll wither and die in prison inside a year. They always do, those Indians.

A week after the trial I took Carlene out for a test drive to make sure she liked the way the Studebaker handled before I put my money down. Tommy Kincaid, the dealer, says, "You all take whatever time you need to get to know this beauty, Sheriff." We headed out 98 along the canal to Twenty-Mile Bend. Carlene got hold of her kerchief under the chin and stared straight ahead and every once in a while she said, "Slow down, Henry, please. My hair." Then she'd sit even straighter and wipe her damp cheek on the shoulder of her white blouse.

At Twenty-Mile, I pulled to the shoulder and switched off the ignition. Carlene sat silently. I examined the dashboard and gripped the steering wheel. We watched a gray carpet of field rats ascend from a drainage ditch and swarm across the highway onto a cornfield. Away across the field, we saw a sharecropper and his children hoeing along a row.

"Well, what do you think, Carlene?"

She looked at the hands folded in her lap. I looked at them. I almost touched them.

"Happy anniversary, sugar," I said.

"I don't want it," she said.

"But honey." I said, "this ain't trash, this is a Studebaker."

"I'd rather have a Maytag," she said.

"But you can't ride in a Maytag," I said.

She said, "Wherever would we go, Henry? It's just swamp and more swamp."

I mentioned maybe Boynton Beach or Tallahassee. Said we might could spend our anniversary weekend in one of those hideaways along the lake.

"Don't," she said. Carlene gripped the hem of her dress with both hands. "Take me home now, Henry."

At the house I told Carlene to go ahead and order the washer from Sears and Roebuck, gave her a peck on the cheek, and said I was going for a ride. I drove for Pahokee.

All this complaining about the cruiser, then, had been Carlene's way of telling me—without having to say it—that she didn't want to go driving at all. Only she didn't want to hurt my feelings, didn't want to admit that staying in the house is more important than stepping out with me. I should have seen that, should have read between the lines, guessed that her way of leaving the swamp is to hide in the house she shared with the two husbands and the child who'd left her.

I've known this about Carlene from the first—that all she ever does is care for people. It's almost her job, how she finds meaning in life. If I were gone, say, she'd have to find someone else to take care of, or she'd die. But she's afraid to have a person care for her except in that vague, Christian way like they do at church. Given her matrimonial history, you can understand her caution, maybe. If someone cares for you and then leaves, that's naturally

worse than a stranger leaving, isn't it? But on the other
hand, when folks leave, they can't hurt you anymore, and
that in turn makes them easier to love, I guess. But what
I've gone and done is force Carlene to acknowledge some-
thing she did not want to. I wish I hadn't. As I drove, I
thought about her back home looking through her photo
album again. She'll wind up all sweet and quiet, out on
the back porch, rocking dreamily, and staring into the
sugarberry tree.

In Pahokee, I parked across from the Flamingo on Lake
Street. Looks like a lot of motels built after the war—L-
shaped, yellow brick, flat roof, red doors with black num-
bers. Gonzalla's final room was Room 6. Out on the street
a fifteen-foot formerly neon flamingo stands in a plot of
weedy earth bordered by boulders painted white. To see it
now, shabby like it is, broken rain gutters, littered lot, and
such, you wouldn't recognize it as the symbol of optimism
it was in 1946 when land speculators and developers tripped
over each other trying to buy up any moderately dry plot
they could find hereabouts. Take a look at the postcards
on the registration desk and you'll see how immaculate
and confident it looked then.

I sat in that car watching and waiting for answers. I
watched for maybe ten minutes. I saw a cloud of sulfur-
colored moths rise up from the castor-bean plant growing
against the side of the office. I saw Mr. Patel, the Paki-
stani owner, walk toward Room 4 with a stepladder and a
garden hose. I saw him kick open the door and go in. You're
a sheriff long enough, you begin to notice details like the
Dodge pickup with the Virginia tags parked at the office
door. Details that might unexpectedly turn into trouble or

suddenly help you solve a mystery. I noticed a blue-vinyl-
and-chrome chair outside Room 12, the heat shimmering
off the roof and off the cracked asphalt of the parking lot,
a child's red tricycle on its side at the top of the trash bin.
Gonzalla, what drove you from your family's arms to this
motel again and again?

You're a sheriff long enough, you realize that every
criminal has a motive, every man has his reasons. You don't
know what it means to want so intensely that you let your
children eat dirt while you make time with your old man.
You can't figure that kind of desperation, maybe, but you
know there is some terrible logic at work, the kind that
frees a person to do what he is impelled to do.

At the Flying A, I check the oil and the radiator, fill it
with ethyl, and drive north, not to anywhere really, just
north away from the heat and the silence and the inevita-
ble dampness. Vanished is what they'll say. Been under a
lot of pressure or something. Someone will remember
Daddy and how he blew out his brains in the lobby of Mr.
Heflin's Belle Glade Five Cent Savings Bank, and they'll
shake their heads. Drive for two days clear to Gatlinburg.
See the Atomic Diner shaped like a big mushroom cloud,
but that's as close as I get to Mam. She never thought I'd
come looking for her. That's how crazy she was. So crazy
she up and left her husband and child and started a new
life simply because the old one was intolerable. Drive so
far north I see snow for the first time and sight my first
penguin. Of course, I don't do any of this. I stare at the
Flamingo. Then at the backs of my hands. Then back at

the motel. I'm not crazy like Mam was or Daddy even. I'm steady. No one will ever have to remember me because I'll be here.

There's a pot of black-bean soup simmering on the stove and a note Scotch-taped to my bowl. "Take your medication," it says. "Beer's in the icebox. I've gone to bed with a headache. Love, Carlene." I put her note in the cookie jar with the others. We've been together these four years and we still don't talk much. I thought it would get easier. Instead, she's learned to write notes, considerate and tender notes, and to get migraines. I've learned to stay at work and let this ulcer burn a hole in my stomach. It's the best we can manage, but it's all right. I mean that. We have come to depend on each other to be cautious and deliberate and distant. We know we are living on perilous ground that might sink as surely as it rose.

I turn off the burner under the soup, undress in the bathroom, and tiptoe to bed. Carlene has her back to me. I know her eyes are open, but I don't let on. I clear my throat, give her a chance to toss, turn, pretend she has woken. And what would I say if she did? I'd say, Carlene, a person would know if his mother were dead, wouldn't he? Mam would be seventy-something now. I picture her sometimes rocking by a fire with the radio tuned to a soap opera. But I don't like to think about that. I close my eyes—I'm eleven or twelve and I'm with my mother and our whole lives are ahead of us. We're on a snowy mountain in Tennessee on the roof of the country; Mam's holding me to keep me from falling.

HARD TIME
THE FIRST TIME

Speedo

Sounds like a bad idea, doesn't it? There I was about to approach my wife of twenty-two years and several months, a woman I still cherished, mind you, even though we had never consummated our love, approach her with the suggestion that she leave her boyfriend, return to me, settle down, and help me parent this overweight, thirty-eight-year-old, slightly retarded roommate of mine. I had it all figured out. It would be a new beginning for the three of us, a final chance at salvation before we all slide into our dotage without having made anything of our lives. We could move out of the city, maybe to Grafton, still on a bus line, but away from the distractions of downtown Worcester. We could rent a cottage by the Wyman-Gordon plant. Eugene would have a yard and Maddy could have a room of her own. I'd plant a garden. We'd be a family. There's nothing wrong with living a normal life. That's all I'm trying to do.

Until I was in seventh grade, I lived that normal life. My mother shopped, cooked, and made me wear rubbers to school. My father laid cable for the electric light company, and I got A's in geography and C's in arithmetic at St. Stephen's School. On special occasions, like First Communion or a birthday, we went out to eat at Messier's Diner. Once in a while we'd vacation at Nantasket Beach. Then my father left us and moved to Tahiti with Donna Mungavon's mother. Never said a word. One night he's lying on the couch watching *The Naked City* on TV, the next afternoon he's on a plane to paradise. Something must have dawned on him. He left us a note. The part to my mother said how he knew this was the best thing for all of us and how he couldn't deny his real passions and like that. The part to me just said, "Get yourself a trade." We never heard from him again.

Mom took a job waitressing at the new Holiday Inn and on Friday nights she'd bring home a salesman. Whoever he was, he'd wear a beige trench coat and black wing-tipped shoes. And he'd ask me about the Red Sox. Guys that date your mother think all you want to talk about is sports. I got so uncomfortable with the long silences and with Mom's laughter that I started staying over my friend

Cooch O'Hara's house, which was also O'Hara's Funeral Home, his dad being the Irish mortician in the neighborhood. One night Cooch brought me to the basement, to his father's studio, he called it, and let me touch Eddie Duffy's corpse. Eddie was our friend who had gotten locked in an old refrigerator at the dump and had died several days before the cops found him. Cooch gave me a long steel clawlike tool and told me to be careful. I pressed on Eddie's chin; maggots bubbled from his mouth. You don't forget a thing like that.

That's when I decided if I lived a holy life, maybe my body would stay together like St. Anthony's and not rot. I ran for president of the St. Dominic Savio Club at school. This, of course, was not normal. Normal people vote or don't vote. Show-offs run for office. I told the students on election day that I had dreamed of carrying the Eucharist through an angry mob of nonbelievers. I promised that if I won, I would pray for each of them when I entered the seminary. I lost to Monica Hebert and forgot about the priesthood.

As a child you have certain uninformed expectations. You assume that you will mature into someone special, say, like your father or like James Dean or John Kennedy, someone unlike the fat men in T-shirts yelling at their kids there in your neighborhood. The fact that there is only one James Dean and a thousand fat men does not influence your thinking one bit. Then something happens like you lose a seventh-grade election or you don't make the high school team, and you realize that maybe you are not so special as you think, but at least you're alive and don't have maggots, and so you set your sights a bit lower and you decide to settle for the small pride of a handsome garden, a tidy house, a sweet wife, and adorable children. Which is sort of what I had in mind when I married Maddy O'Loughlin.

Maddy

There are eight million stories in the naked city, and every one of them is about the same thing—trouble. Trouble doesn't just start when someone wants something he doesn't have. It begins when he decides to do something to get what he doesn't have. I married Maddy in 1965. I was seventeen and had just quit trade school because I was forced out of cabinetmaking and into auto mechanics by my guidance counselor, Mr. Tripodi. Maddy was twenty-one and worked as a baby-sitter at the Town & Country Bowl out on Route 9. In those days I went bowling three mornings a week and had a 175 average. Maddy had already been married twice. At seventeen she married a heavy-equipment operator from Brockton, but that didn't work out. She left him when he punched her in the mouth at the Braintree Ramada Inn in front of his buddies. When she was nineteen, Maddy married a shoe salesman at Kinney's, not knowing that he was already married to a salesgirl at Casual Corner. And here it was an odd-numbered year again.

At four-fifteen on April 30th at City Hall, I in my charcoal-gray continental suit and pink shirt, and Maddy in her Kelly-green minidress became Mr. and Mrs. from that day forward. We drove Maddy's Buick to Mr. Lucky's

Hideaway Motel in Woonsocket, Rhode Island, for our honeymoon. Room 10—I still have the receipt in a cigar box in my room. "That's the bridal suite, you two love-birds," Mr. Lucky's blue-haired wife told us.

Maddy and I had the honeymoon jitters. She was old enough to buy liquor and we ended up drinking too much Tango. By Sunday night, we had been asked to leave two restaurants, I had a tattoo on my left forearm, and Maddy's face was bruised and swollen from when she had fallen down the stairs into Chin's Canton Pagoda. The next morning at the bowling alley Maddy said she never wanted to see me again. She said this out loud in front of Stuart Simone, who ran the pro shop and I know had his eyes all over her. I said, "Come with me, Maddy." She said what was in it for her? I said a house, well, not right away, but when I get work, and a garden, appliances. "That's not what I mean," she said. Stuart smiled. She must have told him about the honeymoon.

Listen, I'll be the first one to tell you that I'm not in the sexual swing of things. I don't seem to possess the same hormones that drive other men. Just ask any woman I've gone out with. I did participate in an unusual three months of indiscriminate and frantic sexual activity the summer after Maddy and I split up. That all ended about Labor Day when I admitted to myself that I was unhappy with brief relationships and realized that brevity was exactly what the women had in mind. I was not even a foot soldier in the great sexual revolution everyone talked about in those days.

Maddy apologized about her remarks at the bowling alley. She was just so certain, she said, that this would be the perfect marriage, we got along so well, that when she realized we were sexually incompatible, she was frustrated and angry. I said, well, maybe it was all the tension and alcohol, so we tried a few more times and our inability to squeeze out sparks only made everything worse. The thing was I saw our love as a fairy tale. Maddy, who had long red hair and cornflower-blue eyes to start with, was like my Sleeping Beauty or Snow White or whoever. I loved her but could not muster the passion that would, in my perverse eyes, defile her.

Maddy let me stay at our place until I figured out what I was doing. We'd stay up late, play gin, talk. She said I was the first guy who ever liked her for herself and not her looks.

"I love your looks."

"You know what I mean, Speedo." Maddy picked from the deck and discarded a jack. "I respect you for that."

"Thanks," I said. "But that's kind of normal, isn't it?" I took the jack. "Maybe you've just been going out with jerks."

"I finally get a guy who loves me, and all I can think about is being seduced by anyone else."

"Thanks, Maddy."

She cried and I told her it was okay, I was sorry. I touched her hand.

"It doesn't make any sense, I know that," she said. "But that's the way it is. Gin."

I figured that eventually Maddy's sexual edge would wear smooth and we'd get back together and be happy. We even talked about going to Europe together when we were old. We liked each other's company.

Eugene

It's normal to look for a person to fill what's empty in your life. It might be someone to love you or someone to take care of you, someone for you to love and care for, or it might be someone who could explain the world to you and your place in it. I think I was looking for someone who would forgive me for screwing everything up. A lot of people with that insight would turn immediately to Jesus, who seems to fit the description rather well. But I was looking for someone more my size, someone who would talk back.

I first met Eugene Bourassa during the Vietnam War when I was a conscientious objector assigned to the Worcester County House of Correction. The Selective Service liked to put us draft dodgers in prisons or hospitals, where they figured we belonged anyway. I worked in the cafeteria cooking starchy meals, watching guards quite openly steal whatever they could from the kitchen, and slopping wet mounds of mystery meat onto inmates' plates. I was nearly through my two years' duty when Eugene appeared in the chow line with his face blue and contused. That meant he was up on a morals offense and had been welcomed by the deputy sheriff.

I found out that Eugene had an IQ in the eighties and spent seven years in the ungraded class at Rice Square School. He was twenty-one then in 1970, lived in a half-way house, and he may not have been smart, but he had the usual needs. Unfortunately, the prostitute he was caught with was only thirteen. I knew the jail's chaplain from antiwar demonstrations, spoke with him, and he managed to get Eugene a cell in protective custody, which meant the rats and screws who wanted to hurt him would have a tougher time getting to him. When I left the job, I continued seeing Eugene the two times a month he could have visitors.

Most people looked at him and thought that Eugene was dangerous. He was short, only five feet, and round, and he had tiny dark eyes, a pointed nose, and absolutely no hair on his body. I'll tell you about the baldness and why he always wore this ball cap with "Structural Cement" printed on the front.

When Eugene was four years and five months old, a tornado tore through the housing project where he lived. That was in 1953 right here in Worcester. Eugene told me about watching a black panther lamp leap off the Motorola and explode through the living-room window, and about a mahogany bureau that flew over his head, hovered like a feather, and then battered through the bedroom wall. Eugene told me about how he found his father, Al, beneath the family's Hotpoint refrigerator. The refrigerator was on the front stoop. Al clutched an orange in his right fist. His head was opened above the nose and the cranial material had been sucked out. So Eugene keeps his hat on, says it holds his head together. When Eugene awoke the morning after the tornado in the Catholic Charities shelter, all of his hair—head, eyelashes, wrists, all of it—was on the bed.

Eugene was paroled on a Tuesday in July after serving a year and a half. He called me to say he'd come by that Thursday and what number apartment was it again. I told him the Vendome Apartments, number 312, write it down.

I told him you could stand at the door of the Alice and the Hat Diner, look up to the third floor, and there's my bedroom window. Eugene didn't make it, though. He got picked up for a parole violation that Wednesday while he was at the Union Pharmacy drinking egg creams with the now fifteen-year-old prostitute who had been the start of his troubles. He served out the remaining year of his sentence.

You've got a city full of honorable citizens living in clean homes, driving cars to jobs and malls, joining one civic or social club or another—doing the accepted and expected. Once in a while, one of them will do something extraordinary, like a young mother will steal a blouse from Filene's or a realtor might try to smuggle a gold watch through customs or something. And if one is caught, there is shame, remorse, perhaps a fine, and a second chance. And that's as it should be in the normal world. If your city councillor is having an affair with some doctor's wife, you might gently suggest that he not run for reelection. Or maybe the United Way's top fund-raiser has inexplicably purchased a condo in Hyannis just as a discrepancy in the books appears, or your President is peddling guns to Latin American death squads. Remember, everyone has his reasons and we all learn from our mistakes. Show mercy.

You've also got an undercity crammed with people like Eugene, people without work, often without the promise of a meal, who live in doorways and parks or crash in shelters and so on. People who can't dress attractively and can't always think lucidly. And every once in a while, one of them will do something crazy, like pay for sexual favors. And if one is caught, it's hard time the first time.

Two weeks after his release, Eugene was arrested for bothering the prostitutes on Piedmont Street. One of the ladies called the cops, incredibly enough. The charge was something like creating a public disturbance, and then you add resisting arrest because Eugene ran when he saw the cruiser turn down Chandler Street. All he did was run into the Shabazz Sandwich Shop and pretend he'd been sitting there for like the last two hours.

At his trial, a shrink from the City Hospital Mental Health Clinic testified that Eugene was addled, but harmless, and his emotional difficulties probably began on the day he found his father, opened the fist, and ate the orange. Despite the doctor's evaluation, his statement that Eugene would not harm a soul, Judge Alden Thayer, son of the very justice who supervised the killings of Sacco and Vanzetti, by the way, called Eugene a dangerous pervert and a singular threat to the young women of the community. His Honor sentenced Eugene to six months back at Worcester County.

So when Eugene got out of jail after serving two months and getting beaten up three times, I met him at the front door and we called a cab to take us to this halfway house on Main Street that was full of real crazies, dopers and other bad examples, and was only blocks from the main cruising area of the city. He said he didn't mind really. It was better than jail. But I told him, Eugene, I got plenty of space in my room, move in with me, which he did.

Lists

I make lists. Lots of them. Lists like "Things to Be Done
Today" (call the city about the excise tax bill; buy peanut
butter . . .), "Favorite Movies" (*Mean Streets, Mildred
Pierce. . .*), "Worst Nightmares" (the one where my mother
takes me to the Pope and tells him she doesn't know me
is the worst), "Reasons Why Man Can Never Be Happy"
(cannot forget his choices nor forgive his decisions; cannot
sit quietly in an empty room), and so on. Wherever I am
I'll just take out my notebook and make a list. It's one of
the things I do that drove Maddy nuts. Others were: read-
ing the newspaper from back to front; flushing the toilet
before using it; saying, "I haven't the slightest idea" and—
well, enough of that. But making lists is how I sift through
all the world's information and how I learn about myself.
There's a point to this.

When Eugene came to live with me back then in 1974,
I knew my job was to keep him out of jail or they'd kill
him the next time. I've seen it happen. Some guard at mess
announces, "We got this kiddie-diddler being transferred
down to 41 North Minimum at two-fifteen, and maybe a
couple of you guys might want to clean out his cell before
he arrives," and he asks for volunteers and so on. You get
the picture. Cell door opens; blanket covers the head; lead
pipe breaks the teeth; and jagged piece of license plate
goes up the ass. They call it bundling. I began to consider
methods for keeping Eugene on the straight and narrow,
so to speak. I hit on the idea of daily self-improvement
lists for him with suggestions like "Don't watch the Lazarro

girl jump rope," and "Don't chew on your finger," and "Don't make that weasel face; it scares people," and like that. But every morning after Pop-Tarts, Eugene would point his binoculars through the Venetian blinds across the street at the kids making their way to Chandler Street School. I was worried. I made another list, "Normalizing Eugene," items numbered 1 to 12, starting with "Take a Long Trip" and ending with "A Mother's Touch."

Sometimes a fresh vantage point will give you a new and enlightening perspective on your life and its prospects. That's what I hoped this trip would do for Eugene. Besides, it was December in New England, and nothing deadens the spirit like ankle-deep slush, steel winds, and pewter skies. I wrote my cousin Remy in Everglades City, Florida, and told him we were coming. A few weeks in the sun, fishing, swimming, eating oysters—I figured that might convince Eugene that there's more to life than teenaged girls.

We caught a one-A.M. coach out of the Greyhound Terminal downtown, which, by the way, is where Perry Smith was arrested as a vagrant just before he murdered that Kansas farm family. You'd know that if you read *In Cold Blood,* but you wouldn't know that a young Eugene Bourassa was picked up in that same sweep for being a "Child in Need of Services." In other words, what was a juvenile doing at midnight alone in the bus depot on a school night?

I hadn't seen Remy since the *Sgt. Pepper* album came out. The last thing we did together was sit in his room listening to "Fixing a Hole" and trying to figure out what it meant. I guess Remy found the answer after I left, because a week later he quit Worcester State College and hit the road in a VW microbus.

From the looks of it, Remy led a comfortable life. He lived alone in an old tin-roofed cracker house on the Barron River and he owned this twenty-five-foot powerboat equipped with radar, tuna tower, outriggers, and flying bridge. He kept the boat docked out behind the house. A more comfortable life than we realized. Remy, we learned, was not a charter boat captain at all. He didn't even fish. He did what everyone else in that town seemed to be doing. He smuggled drugs in and out of the Ten Thousand Islands. Here he was, a high school graduate in work clothes and rubber boots with a four-million-dollar stock portfolio. (He would later become a director of Florida's leading savings and loan association.) Anyway, smoking reefer on the veranda and hiding from the Coast Guard on Chokoloskee Island were not the kinds of therapy I had in mind for Eugene. Remy was sure sorry to see us go. We moved on to #2 on my list: Night School. Can you see my thinking here? "Get yourself a trade." Remember?

Backsliders

At the time of my bright idea, Eugene and I had been roommates for thirteen years. We were renting a furnished two-bedroom apartment over a sporting goods store on North Main. This was the "redeveloped" Worcester that now looked like any Eastern European provincial capital. From our parlor window, we could see the new police sta-

tion, the Centrum, and the phone company's Commu-
nications Center, all built in the windowless, Soviet-inspired
Riot Renaissance style. By that time, Eugene and I had
settled into an uneasy routine. By "routine" I mean we
were both working regularly, me as a housepainter for
Bowditch and Marinelli, Eugene as a janitor at St. Vin-
cent's Hospital. By "uneasy" I mean I still couldn't relax
when Eugene was late for supper or not home by mid-
night.

For a long while there, Eugene had been satisfied with
one or another of his substitutes for young girls. These
included #'s 4, 6, and 11 on my list: bowling (candlepin),
religion (Charismatic Catholic), and for the last five years,
food (sweets and meats). Left alone, Eugene would eat
until he got sick. He was like a goldfish that way. I tried
to limit his intake, but still he put on fifty pounds, and his
coworkers nicknamed him Michelin because he looked like
that cartoon tire man. But since they don't arrest you for
overeating yet, I didn't worry all that much. What did bother
me was that Eugene had recently had a few relapses into,
shall we say, street-legal love. Fortunately, he had not been
arrested. This was 1987. Eugene was thirty-eight, I was
thirty-nine, we had gone through eleven of the twelve items
on my list, and I lived with the knowledge that Eugene
would eventually and inevitably wind up back in jail. And
then where would I be?

When I heard his key in the door, I switched off the TV
set, checked my watch for the time (it was two-fifteen A.M.),
crossed my arms, and sat back on the sofa. "Eugene," I
said when he walked in, "I've been worried sick. Where
have you been?"

"I brought you home some Chinese, Speedo." He held up a white box by its silver handle. "Pork fried rice."

"I know where you've been." I asked him if he liked jail.

He told me he was going to bed and dropped the box onto the coffee table. "You're not my father," he said.

"We have to talk. Sit down," I said. "Please."

Eugene removed his hat, slid the sweatshirt over his head, put the hat back on, and sat by me on the sofa with the sweatshirt balled up in his lap.

So what was I supposed to tell him? To join the Audubon Society, go on the bird walks, meet some mature, sensitive women who'd certainly be dying to sleep with him? Send his picture to Computer Mates with a note, "Under eighteen need not apply"? It's like telling some ghetto kid not to sell drugs, to go back to that underfunded school with the overworked teachers, give up the clothes and meals for a while, and then someday you can work at Burger King or maybe drive a bus, and then you can move out of the project into some nice, clean black neighborhood. Drugs are all he's got.

So I said, "When are we going to stop living day to day?" and I realized how ridiculous that sounded.

Eugene stared at me. "What else is there?"

"I mean, when do we start planning for our futures?"

"Next time."

"Come again?"

"I'm hungry."

"Did you say 'next time'?"

"It's too late this time."

"Eugene, there is no next time. This isn't rehearsal. Is that what you think? On opening night you'll have hair and I'll have confidence. Look at me, Eugene. This is it. You got to get it right the first time."

Which, of course, I hadn't done, not with my parents, not at school, and not with Maddy for sure. I was the King of Missed Opportunities. By the way, Maddy was not doing spectacularly well herself. Consider that she had never divorced me. Did that mean that she held out hope for reconciliation? I liked to think so, but probably she knew it would keep her from making a fourth mistake. And who could blame her?

We saw each other frequently. We'd meet for drinks at the Trocadero. Once a month or so we'd go out to eat at the Sole Proprietor and I'd ask Maddy if we were old enough to go to Europe yet. She'd say don't let's talk about age. Sometimes Eugene joined us, although he didn't much like fish. He did like Maddy, though. She reminded him of Aileen or Arleen or Carleen or Colleen (he couldn't remember) O'Malley, a friend of his from Rice Square School who was now a Maryknoll nun. And Maddy liked Eugene. She usually brought along a present for him from the office supply store where she worked, pens, notepads, and like that.

Of all the things to be afraid of (and there are plenty— I'm up to 73 on my list), the future is surely the most curious because it isn't real. It's all made up. The future exists only in our imaginations. Sometimes, though, just a glimpse of it is so scary or uncomfortable that we close our eyes. That's what I was thinking about at the restaurant while Eugene ate two dozen oysters as an appetizer and Maddy talked about Don Juan Brown. Don Juan is this freezer-sized guy who drives the Zamboni at the Centrum and, more importantly, was Maddy's current affair. If the future exists in the imagination, then you could, at least for the moment, imagine it to be anything at all.

I imagined a cold, snowy morning, frost on our kitchen windows and Maddy in a blue chenille robe and nothing else. We're in Wyoming or someplace where it's thirty miles to the next ranch. Eugene must be away or in the bunkhouse dead asleep. Maddy and I are alone. Coffee perks on the stove, radio plays Bird's "Cherokee." I walk up behind Maddy and slide my hand beneath the robe. I knead her breast. She lets me push her to the floor. We don't care that the linoleum's cold. She closes her eyes beneath me. I say, Are you just going to lie there? Do something to me. She giggles.

"What's on your mind, Speedo?" Maddy said.

"What do you and Don Juan talk about, anyway?"

"His kids. Angie, his ex."

"The future?"

"As far ahead as the weekend, maybe."

Our meals arrived. I told Maddy I had a list of all the reasons we should get back together and did she want me to read it. No. I said I also had a list of her eight boyfriends. And did she know that the usual length of each affair—all right, "relationship"—was two years and two months? No. That meant she and Don Juan were living on borrowed time.

"Is that how you're going to live out your life, Maddy?"

"Speedo, be quiet."

"What have you got to show for your life?"

"What do any of us have?" she said.

Eugene said if we weren't going to eat our meals he

would. I gave him my fries. I got up, stood behind Maddy's chair, and gave her a hug. I sat down and said to her we'll probably be arguing just like this when we're in our seventies and sitting in some pub in Kensington. That would be kind of nice, she said.

View Master

Eugene needed a mother's touch. Some attention, limits, reassurance, clean sheets, and hearty meals would maybe once and for all get his mind off schoolgirls and shift his energies into the right gear or at least get him moving in a less dangerous direction. So I would find him a woman who could do a little mothering. I had been avoiding this final item on my list because the only mother I knew was my own, and she was decidedly not the maternal type. She tended bar now at the Sports Page Lounge and dated aging ex–softball players who still talked about the day they went six-for-six against the Interstate Batterymen in 1961 or '62. I shouldn't be sarcastic about these guys; at least they had a moment of accomplishment. What did I have to remember—the night I almost made love to my wife?

The past shouldn't be able to hurt you anymore. I mean, you could bury it, right? But you don't. It's a wormy corpse that you keep around the house and stare at. On the first night Maddy and I tried making love after drinking all that Tango, her hair stunk of my cigarettes and I kept struggling, kept pumping, thinking how a tornado can drive a straw through a tree. She watched me work. She tapped my shoulder and asked me what I was doing. She said she was going to be sick. A straw, not a noodle.

"Eugene, where's the View Master?" I wanted to get my mind off my honeymoon. The View Master helps me to relax.

Eugene was at the window with his binoculars. He jerked around, stared at me, and closed one eye as if he were a camera. I love Eugene when he's trying to be funny. He has such an engineer's sense of humor. Eugene bit his lower lip and hummed as he panned the room. He focused on the telephone, which sat on a three-legged table. Beneath the table lay the View Master and a shoebox full of slide reels. "Thank you, Eugene."

The greatest invention of the twentieth century is the GAF View Master. How do they get those three dimensions into two? I don't know. I can tell you this, though, that the reel on Niagara Falls makes it look better than it really is. I've been to Niagara Falls. Do yourself a favor, stay home. Sometimes I slip in a reel and make up a story to go along with the pictures. Take "Colorful San Francisco": Here's Eugene and I eating at Alioto's and discussing our latest caper (click!) and then we speed off to the Embarcadero to foil some CIA operatives who are smuggling cocaine out of Colombia (click!) but they elude our trap and we chase them through Chinatown to an opium den behind the Universal Café (click!) . . . You get the picture. Sometimes I told these adventures to Eugene to get him to sleep at night.

I leaned back on the sofa, pointed the View Master at the ceiling light, and flipped through "Monkey Jungle of Miami." Eugene would have to overcome his attraction to young girls if he were ever to become a normal, upstanding citizen. I agreed with him that youngsters often are more sensitive and understanding than adults, but as I often pointed out, there were legal and even moral considerations to take into account.

And that's when I thought about Maddy. And that's when I should have gone to the movies or to the Y for a steam bath. I could have walked upstairs and had a cup of tea with Mr. Presley (no relation), but instead I lay right there on the couch staring at a blue-faced mandrill, smiling to myself, and thinking I had solved the problem. I wish I had thought a little harder.

Thursday night is hockey night at the Centrum, which meant that Maddy would be meeting Don Juan at the Trocadero around nine. I told Eugene to take a shower. I've got a surprise, that's why. I took a sponge bath myself, tied my hair back in a ponytail, put on a white shirt and this cowboy string tie that I knew Maddy liked. I laid out Eugene's sport coat, his tan chinos, and a polo shirt. All the to-do made Eugene suspicious. The only time he ever wore that sport coat was to the courthouse. But I assured him he was not under arrest.

"So what's the deal, Speedo?"

"You'll see. We're just going out to a club like regular people. Now get dressed."

"I won't."

"We're going to see Maddy, that's all. I've got a plan."

Eugene sat on the floor and crossed his arms.

I never could keep a secret anyway. I told him what I had in mind, but the revelation only made him more anxious. He began to moan like he does. I told him tonight we would have to impress Maddy enough so that she would want to come and take care of us.

"Like Wendy Darling?"

"Right, Eugene."

"We're the Lost Boys?"

I thought about it. "I guess we are."

Eugene dressed. I straightened his collar. He asked if he could take the View Master. He wore it around his neck like a camera and stuffed his coat pocket with a dozen or so reels. I called a cab.

Maddy sat in a booth by herself nursing a Rum Coke and reading a paperback. She wore wire-frame glasses. We said good evening.

"Well, aren't you two spiffy. What brings you out into the night?"

"Are those bifocals?"

Maddy took off the glasses, closed the book. "You didn't come here just to remind me I'm getting old."

"No," I said. "We want to talk. But let me get drinks."

Buzzy Notorangelo was the only other customer in the lounge. He was trying to read the racing form in the blue light of the TV. Miss Delores slept on her bench at the end of the bar. Miss Delores is Shampoo's mother. Shampoo's the bartender. Miss Delores is in a nursing home now, but in those days she was still living with her son. She was too flighty for Shampoo to leave her at home, she wandered off, so he took her to work. It was considered good luck at the Trocadero to rub Miss Delores's stockinged feet on the way to the men's room. I ordered a Rum Coke and two beers. Buzzy asked me to read a horse's name in the tenth at Rockingham. Crested Beaut, I said. That's her, he said.

"Maddy, we've got a proposition for you."

"I've heard that before."

"We're good people come on hard times, right? I've got a plan that will make life better for the three of us."

"The three of us?"

"Yes."

"Speedo, Don Juan'll be here in like five minutes and he's taking me to the Queen Elena for steamers."

"This won't take long."

Eugene slid a reel into the View Master and was mumbling a narrative as he clicked through it. I heard him say "Neverland." Maddy took out a compact mirror and looked at her face.

"I've got a plan that's going to save us all."

"Who needs to be saved?"

"You, for one."

"From what?"

I looked around us. "From this," I said. "Where are you going, Maddy?"

"I told you. To the Queen Elena."

"You know what I mean. With your life."

"I'm happy with my life."

Anyway I told her what I had in mind. "I'm going to buy a house, or rent one, I don't care. A nice place out in the country sort of. And I want the three of us to live there. You won't have to pay rent. You could quit work if you want."

Maddy stared at me. "What do you think you're doing?"

"Oh, I know what you're thinking. No way. Separate

rooms. You can have Don Juan over if that's what you want."

"Excuse me for saying so, Speedo, but I think you're going crazy."

"What the hell is crazy about wanting a family?"

"Is that what you call a family? No offense, but come on. A husband and wife who sleep in different rooms and have dates stay over? A child practically the parents' age?"

"I know it doesn't sound right, but it's more family than we've got."

"Families are for the young, Speedo. They've got the energy and the time for it."

We heard a horn from the street. "That'll be Don Juan," Maddy said and gathered her things. "Thanks for the drinks, Speedo. Bye, Eugene."

I grabbed her wrist. "So what do you live for, Maddy?"

"That's a silly question. You just live."

"You're a goddam loser, Maddy, you know that."

"Speedo, let go of my hand."

"Let go, Speedo," Eugene said.

"No, I won't. I want you, both of you, to face it. We're three losers here."

"You're hurting me. I'll scream."

Eugene pulled at my arm. I slapped him in the face. And then I felt it. Eugene hit me square on the eyes with the View Master. And I'm told he hit me again and again until Buzzy pulled him off me. I woke up on top of the bar, a jacket under my head and a bloodied bar rag on my face. "You'll be all right," Shampoo said. "Eugene went on home."

Last Looks

Two years later, on December 3, 1989, Eugene Bour-
assa, aged forty years and ten months, was discovered dead
in his cell in North Minimum at the Worcester County
House of Correction. I found that out a week later when I
arrived for my visit. The story wasn't in the papers. These
things never are. The county buried him at Hope Ceme-
tery without even calling me, like I was nobody. One of
the guards told me that Eugene had made a rope of braided
bedding and had hanged himself from a ceiling pipe. I
was glad to hear that. At the last minute, Eugene had taken
control of his life, deprived the bastards of their little plea-
sure.

The sheriff, who had been the deputy assigned to wel-
coming sex offenders back in the old days, refused to give
me any of Eugene's possessions until I hired a lawyer, and
then the sheriff said they couldn't find anything, that they
had no records of any personal property belonging to
Eugene Bourassa. Not the tape deck I had given him the
day he was locked up, not the View Master, nothing. I
wanted the hat, that's all.

Maddy came with me to the grave. She said she was
sorry. She was. There we were at four in the afternoon, in
the dark and the sleet, each with an armful of plastic flow-
ers, standing over Eugene's granite marker.

"You were his savior, Speedo," Maddy said.

"You don't know anything about it, Maddy. Not the first
thing."

"You can't blame yourself for this."

"I want a divorce."

We didn't even fight about it. I told her I had a lawyer now. If she wanted, we could share her. We caught a bus back to the city. I felt different, lighthearted, the way I always imagined other people felt when I saw them laughing in public places. I had a new past now and I liked it. I started a list in my head of things I needed to do: call Remy, get a haircut, visit Mom, paint the apartment. I looked at Maddy staring out the window into the sleet. Her hair was wet and a curl stuck to her cheek.

PEOPLE THAT DREAM, WHALES THAT DANCE

JULIAN'S NOT SURE what he's looking for, but he says he'll know it when he feels it. Julian's my father and we've been living here in Cabin 7 at the Harbor Lights Motor Inn since early May. These three months in Provincetown are the longest time we've stayed in one place in quite a while. We came here after a rainy month at the Silver Horseshoe Motel in Memphis, Tennessee. Before that Julian was a sign painter in Eureka, Kansas. We lived at Falconetti's Motor Lodge until a twister lifted off the building's corrugated roof. Julian and I have traveled through forty-five states and have lived in seventeen in just the last four and a half years.

Fernando—he's the boy I'm going to tell you about—is the first friend I've ever had who is my own age. Usually, it's just been me and Julian, or just me and some rickety television, or me and a full-length mirror on a bathroom door. I never stayed in one school long enough to make a friend I could tell stories to or run away with. Before we came here, when Julian would be spot welding at a ship-yard or installing rain gutters or whatever, I'd have to sit in the motel room and make up people to play with. We'd play games like "School Social Worker." You can play. It's easy.

In "School Social Worker" you pretend that you don't know me, but you need to know my case history. And I pretend I don't want to tell you. Then you tell me to go with my feelings, and you give me a reassuring hug. And then you ask me my name. My name is Chloe Marie Martel-McDonald, I tell you. You act surprised at such a long name, and you make a joke about it. You say you hope I don't marry a boy named Jesse James Lennon-McCartney and decide to give our children both last names. Think of it, you say. It's always the children who suffer. I pretend not to understand your joke or your painful slip of the tongue. You pretend to cough. You ask me my age. Twelve. That was easy. Father's name? Julian Martel. Mother's name? Oh no, you've asked the wrong question. I begin to cry.

But now we're here in P-town, and Julian's tending bar at the Foc'sle on Commercial Street, and I've made a friend named Fernando Augusto. I told Julian that we should stop moving because if we drive any further east we'll fall right off the beginning of the country. Julian laughed.

Our cabin sits back from the road and is surrounded by sand and twisted dwarf pines. It's the closest cabin to the ocean, and all night we can hear the waves splashing on the rocks. A blue wooden table and two blue metal folding chairs stand in the middle of our room. The brown linoleum floor is always a little gritty from the sand that blows through the bruises and cuts in the old screen door. Julian's single bed is by the bathroom and mine is across the room by the closet. We have a small square fridge underneath a two-burner stove. Next to the sink, on the small Formica countertop, are a pop-up toaster and a Juice-O-Matic orange squeezer. I tacked up the sixteen picture postcards of our seventeen homes on the knotty-pine wall over my bed. The Sahara Motel in Dewitt, Arkansas, didn't even have postcards. Julian placed his photograph in its foldout cardboard frame on a shelf over the sink. It's a hand-tinted color college graduation picture of my mother.

My mother has eyes as blue as motel swimming pools and hair as red as neon. I have Julian's sandy hair, his green eyes, and his long, thin nose, but I got my high cheekbones, the space between my front teeth, and my first name from my mother. When he first met my mother, Julian says, they were both in college and were planning to be high school English teachers. At first, she would never tell him who she was or what she did. Julian says my mother was a born actress and was always on stage. One day, for instance, she would pretend to be a registered nurse named Carmen, and then she would be a seamstress named Colette. And then one Thursday morning at geography class, in the middle of a slide presentation on continental drift, she said her name was Chloe. Then she said she'd marry Julian. Her real name, he discovered later, was Zoe McDonald.

Zoe McDonald, housewife by day, became Ariel at night and sang lead for a rock band named the Tempests up near Lodi. One day she stayed Ariel, left Julian and me, and ran away to Los Angeles with the band. Julian says that nobody can shine brighter than Hollywood lights. I was seven and a half years old when we hit the road. I hardly remember Modesto.

But I do remember this one morning in May that my mother came to JFK Elementary and had me called out of arithmetic class. This was shortly before she left us. When I walked into the principal's office, Zoe was sitting on the detention bench talking in hushed tones with Dr. Cipro. Zoe told him that my Aunt Marilyn, her own identical twin, was dying over in Turlock. She gave me a hug. Marilyn had some rare kind of Eastern European bone-marrow disease, Zoe said, and was asking to see me, her only godchild, at her deathbed. Dr. Cipro said he was sorry to hear about Marilyn. It's worse than cancer, Zoe told him. Dr. Cipro stood. He said of course I'd be excused for the day, and he shook Zoe's hand. Thank you so much, she said. She put on her sunglasses, sniffled, took my hand, and we left school.

Only I don't have an Aunt Marilyn.

"Did you have to say she was dying?" I asked.

Zoe laughed. "Did you see how he kept fiddling with his cufflinks?"

"Now he's going to want to know what happened."

"Tell him she died."

"Great."

"And then just cry anytime he mentions it."

For a while we just drove around listening to Zoe's Van Morrison tapes. First to the airport and then on the freeway almost to Salida. I asked her what was going on.

"Do I need a reason to want to see my daughter?" she said.

I said, "I think so."

"Okay. I got lonely when you went to school. How's that?"

We ended up at a café off McHenry Avenue called Pookie's. We sat on green vinyl chairs at a white table. A man with a straw cowboy hat read the newspaper at the counter. Zoe ordered beer and nachos. I had a date milk shake, which I love, and a bean burrito. Zoe kept staring at me while I ate. Someone in the kitchen sang along to a radio.

"Are you okay?" I said.

"Perfect."

"So how come we're here?"

"Thought I'd spring you for the day, that's all." Zoe reached across the table and swept a string of hair behind my ear. She said, "Don't you ever want to play hooky, stop being Miss Brain Wave for a day and just have fun?"

"I don't want to get into trouble."

"Sometimes you'll go crazy if you keep doing what everyone wants you to do. You'll see."

I didn't know what she was getting at, but I could see she wanted me to say something. I said we can't just do whatever we want, can we? She laughed and said I sounded like her mother, and she said, no, we can't have everything we want. I found out later that was true.

Fernando lives in the West End in a white bungalow with moss-green shutters. The house sits behind a white picket fence that's covered with pink and yellow roses. Fernando is an only child like me. His father is captain of the *Isabella* and his mother cooks linguica and squid in their fragrant little kitchen. When she cooks, she listens to opera played softly on the radio. Sometimes Fernando and I sit there at the kitchen table. We'll eat chowder and Mrs. Augusto will say something in Portuguese to Fernando and he'll blush, and we'll all smile. The sun will slant through the window; the wind will lift a starched curtain so it brushes my arm, and I'll feel like I've sat there all my life and I won't want to leave.

When school starts in September, Fernando says, we'll be in the same grade, but I tell him I don't know if I'll be around then 'cause Julian might want to go back to Birmingham or Raleigh, or he might want to try someplace new like Ely, Nevada.

"Ely, Nevada," Fernando goes. "Jesus Christ!"

"That's right," I say, and I tell him how Julian and I drove through there three years ago and he noticed that they didn't have a bookstore. Julian is always buying me books since I miss so much school—mostly nineteenth-century novels because he says I'm too young for the twentieth century. Anyway, he figures we could open a bookstore in Ely even though nobody there reads anything but spots on playing cards. Julian figures that if there were good books available, the citizens of Ely would read.

Julian is very naive like that. He says you can't judge a book by its cover, but you can judge a person by his books. Julian always says you are what you read, so the first thing he does in every motel room is toss out the Gideon Bible. Let's not take any chances, he says. Julian is very whimsical like that. If Julian's right, if you are what you read, then he's a map, and I'm a handsome, clever young woman possessed of an inordinately comfortable home and radiantly cheerful disposition. I love Jane Austen.

Fernando's so cute. He's got nut-brown eyes, black hair that he ties back in a ponytail, and one dimple when he smiles. He's as thin as a minute. And he knows everything you need to know about P-town. He knows how to finagle the alley door to the Wharf Cinema so we can sneak into the movies. Every Wednesday is Bogart night. Fernando says that he loves movies even more than he loves boats. Fernando knows all the skippers of the sport-fishing boats and can always get as much free flounder as Julian and I can eat. Fernando knows where in the beech forest the red foxes live. He knows where the ospreys nest at Pilgrim Springs. Fernando even knows a path up to the monument, where, he says, you can always find at least one junkie passed out. In their backpacks, Fernando says, they usually have lots of giftware and jewelry items that they've boosted from the downtown shops. Fernando says that's how he got his gold chain and his diamond earring.

Some days Fernando and I get up at four A.M. and meet down at the Portuguese Bakery and help Mr. Teixeira unload flour and eggs from his Chevy station wagon. Mr.

Texiera gives us a warm loaf of sweet bread and Styro-foam cups of espresso, and we go sit on the benches in front of Town Hall and enjoy our breakfast as the sun rises over the rosy tip of America. And Fernando always says, "We're the first people in the country to see today."

P-town is quiet at dawn. There are no barefooted pedestrians dodging bell-ringing bicycles, no honking automobile horns, and no screams from the drinkers at the streetside bars. Just us and a few black dogs with blue bandannas sniffing and pissing their way along Commercial Street. Just us and an occasional couple of attractive men walking arm in arm, laughing, maybe a little drunk, on their way home from another party.

We sit and eat and Fernando tells me about his plans, about what he wants to do with the rest of his life. Last Wednesday morning Fernando was talking about going to the Cape Verde Islands to see his grandfather when this beautiful man with a halo's worth of blond ringlets falling to his shoulders walks up to us and sits down beside Fernando. The man wore a red shirt, black leather pants, and one red sneaker. He crossed his legs and wiggled the toes of his bare left foot.

"You are a stunning young couple," he said, "and I am overwhelmed, I'm sure, to make your acquaintance."

Fernando and I stared at one another. The man leaned to his left and pulled a red silk handkerchief from his back pocket.

"Allow me to introduce myself. I am Xury, as in Fury, Charles, as in Prince, and Angel, as in Falls, and I am singularly thrilled to be your guest this morning." He unfolded his handkerchief, spit on it, and begging our kind indulgence, began to wash his soiled foot.

"What kind of name is Xury Charles Angel?" I asked him.

"French."

"You don't look French," Fernando said.

"I'm from California," Xury said.

Xury told us that he'd been abandoned by a swarthy somebody with a curiously precise pencil-thin mustache and a black sleeveless T-shirt that said "Let's Dance" on the front. "He left me at the lighthouse last night and when the tide came in, I couldn't make my way across the jetty."

"That's awful," I said. Fernando poked me in the ribs.

"He told me he was a fisherman," Xury said. "I adore sportsmen. May I have a piece of your bread?"

Fernando tore a hunk of bread off the loaf and handed it to Xury.

"He was probably a television anchorman from Hartford," Xury said. "Whatever he was he could certainly dance."

Xury asked if he might have a sip of my espresso. It's cold, I said, but he drank it anyway and said that it hit the spot.

"Do you have any idea what time it is?" Xury asked.

"About six," Fernando guessed.

"Good. I'd hate to be late for work on my last day."

"Where do you work, Xury Charles Angel?" I asked.

"At the Gryphon Bookstore."

"The Gryphon?"

"It's down Commercial," Fernando said. "It's by that bar with the man dressed as a lobster in the window."

"Yes, you can't miss it," Xury said. "Please drop in for a visit. I'll be there till nine tonight, ah . . ."

"Chloe," I told him, "Chloe Marie Martel-McDonald. And this is my friend Fernando."

"Pleased to meet you both." Xury stood up, bowed from the waist, and kissed both our hands. He sat down again and ate more bread. Fernando turned the diamond in his ear. I watched a black dog assault a green trash bag in front of the Stormy Harbor Restaurant. We heard screams. The seagulls were waking up.

That night at supper I asked Julian what a fag was. He said we don't call them fags. I said Fernando does. He said Fernando's just a boy, and he wiped a leaf of wet kale from his chin and told me to eat my soup. I said, Julian, you won't leave me in school long enough to learn these things, so you have to tell me. Julian said homosexuals are people who prefer to love people of their own sex. I said I knew that much. Julian coughed and wiped his lips with a paper napkin. Is that it? I asked him. Julian nodded. So what's wrong with that? Julian shook his head. Nothing, he said. Julian asked if Fernando and I were going to meet him on his break.

"My friend Xury Charles Angel is a homosexual."

"What's a Xury Charles Angel?" Julian asked.

We cleaned off the table and did the dishes. Julian wiped. I walked Julian to work and he held my hand all the way down Commercial Street.

"Julian, why did Zoe leave us?"

"I don't know, honey, I don't know."

"Maybe she wasn't happy."

Julian squeezed my hand.

"I'm just trying to figure it out, Julian," I said. "I suppose she must hate us."

"I don't know."

"We'll probably never know."

"You're probably right, Chloe."

Julian writes to Zoe at least once from every place we stay. He tells her we're doing well, that I've grown another inch, that we miss her, and that he's working things out, whatever he means by that. He asks her how her music career is going and tells her if she needs to reach us she can write to the something-or-other motel in wherever we are. He signs it "Love, Julian" and mails the letters to this record company in Long Beach that nobody's ever heard of.

"Can we burn the picture?"

"Your mother's picture? No, we can't burn the picture."

"Why not?"

"Don't talk foolishly, Chloe."

"Why not, Julian? Why do you build a little shrine for her in every motel room? That's what it is, you know, your little picture on the shelf."

"She's my . . . well, she's your mother."

"I don't even know her, Julian. Neither do you. And anyway, a photograph is not a mother. Or a wife."

"Chloe . . ."

"We won't have to run away from her if we don't keep packing her in a suitcase."

We stopped at the door of the Foc'sle, and Julian told me he had to go in to work.

"I hate her, Julian."

"Please, Chloe."

Julian kissed me. I tightened the knot on his thin red tie and told him I'd be back for his nine-o'clock break. Then I walked to the pier to meet Fernando.

Twice a day, when the Boston boat arrives and departs, Fernando and his friends jump off the pier into the brown, jellyfish-thick water and dive for coins thrown by the tourists. Fernando says he wants to retire. He gets more stings than quarters, he says. But it's expected that all the Portuguese boys in junior high will dive for coins from Memorial Day to Labor Day. Fernando's father says that this picturesque custom delights the tourists and that, he says, is good for Provincetown's economy.

So twice a day, at noon and at six, I walk out to the pier and watch Fernando at work. All the boys look like little marine cyclopes with their face masks on and their heads bobbing in the water. I can always tell Fernando though by the gleam of the gold chain around his neck. Fernando can stay under water for a full minute—longer than any of his friends. His friends don't like me very much. They tease Fernando and say that I'm his girlfriend, and they think it's even funnier because I'm a little taller than Fernando. They won't even talk to me. Fernando says that they're just dumb. Julian says that everyone knows that people who won't say hello to you are just silly and pretentious. They want you to think they know something that you don't know. Julian thinks they're scared. I think they're boring.

I wait while Fernando cleans and changes in the cannery locker room, and then we sit on the pier and count up his wages and decide how to spend the evening. Sometimes we buy saltwater taffy and walk out to Race Point or Herring Cove. Some nights we fish with drop lines off the side of the *Isabella* when she's tied up at the pier. All we ever catch is those ugly sea robins or tiny menhaden. We might go to the movies, or we might just drift up and down Commercial Street with the crowd. Last Wednesday night Fernando and I sat on the wicker swing on the front porch of the Atlantic House. We listened to the music from the disco inside and we talked. When I grow up, Fernando said, I don't want to catch fish. I want to watch whales. Watch them do what? I ask. Dance, he says.

Fernando says you have to go out real early to see the cows and their calves breeching and sounding, not like the tourist boats that leave at eight A.M., he says. And you have to steam out to Stellwagon Bank to see the big humpbacks and fins. I'm just going to take kids and movie stars out on my boat, he goes, no tourists.

"You remind me of Julian," I say. "You're always dreaming."

"You know what I'm going to call her?"

"Who?"

"My boat. I'm going to call her the *Chloe Marie* and you can be my partner."

"Thanks, Fernando," I say. "But I'm worried." I tell him that Julian might be wanting to leave soon. He's been tinkering with the car and unfolding road maps at the dinner table. He sits there, I tell Fernando, and traces his finger along the red lines and then stares out the screen door. Fernando says that his favorite movie is *The African Queen*. Listen, Fernando, I say, if Julian hasn't found what he's looking for then we might not see each other again. Fernando begins yelling about leeches on his legs. I ask him how he'd feel if he never saw me again. Fernando jumps up and leaps off the veranda. I forget, he goes, I have to help a buddy out of a jam. As if I believed him. I'll see you at ten, he yells, and runs off.

I wandered up Commercial Street wondering what I'd do till Julian's break. And then I remembered Xury. I was glad that there were no other customers in the Gryphon, because I wanted to talk. Xury was glad that I had come to visit him because, he said, he'd been reading a distressing article on AIDS in *Newsweek*, and he just couldn't bear to be alone a moment longer.

We sat on folding chairs at a small reading table by the poetry section. Xury said I should smile, things couldn't be that bad.

"Is this really your last night, Xury?"

"Unfortunately. I am expected back at the university on Monday. I teach philosophy, Chloe. Can you believe that?"

"Sure."

"Ideas. Terribly dull stuff, Chloe. Not so interesting as people."

"Or whales."

"Come again?"

"Fernando says whales can dance."

"They do," Xury said and pointed to this poster stapled to a wooden beam in the middle of the store. An acrobatic humpback leaped from the ocean and pointed a great white wing at the crescent moon. Water poured from her flanks like showers of diamonds. Xury told me whales sing, too. Haunting and beautiful songs, he said. I wondered if you could dance to whale music.

A girl carrying her baby in a Snugli walked in and asked directions to the Land's End Inn. She couldn't have been more than seventeen. She said the baby's name was Layla. While Xury took her outside and pointed up Commercial Street, I sat on my leg and stared at the poster.

"So where were we?" Xury said when he sat down.

"Do you know why they dance?" I asked.

"I like to think they're happy about something. In love maybe."

"I dance with Julian sometimes," I said. "Like when we're moving again, Julian will turn on the radio and we'll dance our room goodbye."

I told Xury about the seventeen homes in the four and a half years. I asked him if he knew what would make Julian stop moving."

"You."

"Me?"

I thought for a moment. I told Xury that I was going to meet Julian at nine at the Foc'sle. Xury said maybe he'd see us there. First he was going to go home and suit up for the big game. It's the last night of the season, he said.

Julian was starting his break when I arrived. He offered me half of his clam roll. I said I'd come to talk. Okay, he said and got himself a shot of cognac and me a bottle of Moxie.

"What's wrong, Julian?" I said.

Julian pushed his plate to the side of the table. He wiped his lips and finished chewing. He sipped his cognac. "I don't know, Chloe. I really don't. I don't feel happy."

Julian looked at his glass. Then he looked at me with his big, sad father eyes.

The Foc'sle is a small, dark barroom with long pine tables and benches which are deeply carved with names and initials and little arrow-pierced hearts. The low-beamed ceiling is decorated with bleached starfish and pearly scallop shells. Lobster traps and buoys hang from the fishnets along the brick walls. Suspended over the middle of the bar is a large steering wheel from a schooner, and over the cash register is a wooden plaque made like a ship's nameplate reading *Andrea Doria*. Most of the crew of the *Isabella*, in fact most of the fishermen in P-town, drink at the Foc'sle, and most of them have their wives and children with them.

"Fishermen!" I heard someone yell from the doorway. I turned around and saw him. "Julian," I said, "you are about to meet Xury Charles Angel."

Xury's blond hair sparkled with flecks of red glitter. He wore a silky white Celtics basketball jersey, black leather shorts, white knee socks, and high-cut black sneakers.

"One on one, anybody?" Xury said. Someone coughed. Someone else set a glass down on the bar. A baby sneezed. Someone hit the Spiders-from-Mars-Super-Double-Bonus bell on the Ziggy Stardust pinball machine. I ran to the door and grabbed Xury's hand. Come on, I said, I want you to meet my father.

I pulled Xury along to our little table by the bar and introduced him to Julian. Xury ordered a bottle of cognac for himself and Julian. I declined another Moxie. Xury said he was feeling gloomy and proposed a toast to his last night in Provincetown. He shot down his drink and poured another.

No, it's not because I'm leaving, he told Julian. "AIDS is changing everything up here," Xury said. "Everyone's paranoid. I have to tell guys I'm from Dayton or Little Rock. If they know you're from San Francisco, they won't touch you with a ten-foot cattle prod."

"I saw the piece in *Newsweek*," Julian said.

"What's AIDS, Xury?" I asked.

Julian said, "It's this disease that started in . . ." He looked at Xury. "Africa, right?"

"Right," Xury said. "And spread to Haiti, and from there, they figure, it moved to the States. Mostly it's gays who are dying."

"And there's no cure for it." Julian said.

"Here it is 1984," Xury said, "and we can grow a baby in a bottle, replace a heart with a plastic pump, but we can't treat this." He shook his head.

"What kind of disease?" I asked.

"Merciless," Xury said. "It's a virus that breaks down your immune system, so any old kind of infection could kill you. And it carries a few of its own. Anyway, because it's a virus, it gets into your cells and you can't kill it without killing the cells."

Julian raised his glass. "Here's to medical research."

"I tell you, Julian, P-town is going to end up like Hyannis. You'll never see another sequined dress on Commercial Street. There'll just be fat-bellied men with thin white legs wearing madras bermudas, brown shoes, and John Deere hats, or couples with matching jerseys with their names on the back. The man will carry a camera. The wife will lug a large straw bag. 'I thought you said there were queers here, Frank,' she'll whine. 'Shut your face, Estelle,' he'll say. And when they realize that they have no target for their moral indignation, they'll go back to Keokuk."

I said, "We've been to Keokuk," and smiled at Julian.

"And the restaurants will close and so will the shops. P-town will be left with Norman Mailer, a few fishing boats, and a bunch of tanned backpackers trying to score some hash."

"What are you going to do?" Julian asked him.

Xury shrugged his shoulder. "Maybe I'll get married and settle down. Maybe I'll take winter vacations." He laughed. "It's hard when something you rely on becomes something else."

Maybe Julian heard what I heard, the words "married" and "settle down" tied together in Xury's sentence. Or maybe it was the "something you rely on" that made him uncomfortable. He started twisting the hair behind his ear. Sometimes he pulls it right out.

"*Salut!*" Xury said and downed his cognac. "Everything changes, Chloe, even change." Xury winked at me. "So, Julian, what about you two? Will you be staying here?"

Julian shook his head. "We're not sure. We haven't decided yet."

Xury and Julian toasted the romance of the road and Xury told us how he ran away from home when he was in high school.

"We lived outside Chicago. My father was a county commissioner, and I was an embarrassment to him. He got me in therapy, trying to make a 'man' out of me, as he put it. The shrink was a guy from the country club, Dad's old Air Force buddy, and he kept asking me why I wanted to hurt my parents."

"Enlightened," Julian said.

"Actually, I think he was gay and didn't want to face it. I was a threat." Xury poured an inch of cognac into his glass, drank it, and went on. "Anyway, I was tired of playing family freak, so I ran away, figured I'd punish the old man. I went to Defiance, Ohio, because the name was so appropriately symbolic, and it was about as far as I could stand riding a bus. I sent him a postcard of Independence Dam State Park, which is where I was camping. The name of the park was more than I could have hoped for. I lived in a tent there for two months."

"And then?"

"I was miserable. Half the time it rained. Families in Winnebagos would get to the campsite next to mine and sit up watching TV all night. I never slept. I ate tuna fish every day. The only boys in the campground were either fishing with their fathers or coming on to all the pouty little blond girls."

"So what did you do?"

"One night the tent collapsed in a thunderstorm. I lay there under that nylon shroud, soaked, cold stiff, until morning, and I realized I was the only one getting punished. So I went home. My mother cried, took me to an Italian restaurant, and watched me eat for two hours. They got used to me after a while. My father would manage to

be out when I had a friend over. We learned to get along
that way."

"Happy ending," Julian said.

Didn't Julian get the point, I thought, that you can't run
away from yourself? But I was too tired to say anything.

Xury said he wanted to hear about our travels. I told
him how we always met the most interesting people in
laundromats. Like Lottie Drinkwater, the Cat Lady of
North Augusta, South Carolina. She owned twenty-six
spayed cats, one for each letter of the alphabet, from Annie
to Zelda.

"She had to be ninety years old," Julian said, "and there
she was washing out these twenty-six handmade cat beds."

"Peter was my favorite, though," I said. Peter was a pro-
fessor in Monroe, Louisiana, who had tattoos on both arms
and a rack of nineteen pipes on his kitchen table. Each
pipe was labeled with numbered masking tape, and Peter
smoked them in rotation.

Julian told Xury how when we first met Peter at the
University Washeteria, he was depressed because his min-
ister at the Parkview Baptist Church had left his family
and run off with Peter's twenty-year-old girlfriend. He told
us how for the first time since Vietnam he'd been in love,
how twenty-two years seemed the ideal age difference for
a couple, and so on. Peter thanked Julian for listening to
his problems and invited us to his apartment. We stayed
for a month. Every night I'd fall asleep on the couch while
Julian and Peter talked about poetry. When we left for
Biloxi, Peter was dating this teenaged waitress at the Steak
'n' Egg and making an emotional recovery.

Just then the bell rang for Julian to get back to work. I

told him if we had a house then Peter could come and visit us for a while. He ignored the remark, kissed me on the head, eased himself out from our table, and got back behind the bar. Xury and I moved to barstools and Julian went on telling stories. He laughed about the one day that he was a cowboy in Bozeman, Montana, and I realized that I had never seen Julian talk so fast or smile so quickly. Poor Julian, I thought. He doesn't have a friend his own age, no one to fool around with or talk to. It was nearly ten. I told them both goodbye and walked to Town Hall to wait for Fernando.

"What are you thinking about, Chloe?" Fernando sat beside me. I shrugged. I couldn't tell him because I didn't know the name for how I felt. We just sat quietly with our heads on the back of the bench and stared at the night sky. And then Fernando said look at that cloud; it goes on forever like a dream. My dream's no cloud, I thought. My dream is like a small white cottage. You can see it and touch it. You can even live in it.

"Chloe, look!" Fernando said. Coming down Commercial Street was Xury Charles Angel with his arm around a thin black man who carried a white poodle at his chest. They passed without noticing us. We heard Xury say that he adored computer programmers. They sat on the last bench.

Fernando apologized for leaving me at the Atlantic House. He said I was his best friend and that he would really be sad if I moved away. I said thank you and told him I wanted very much to work on his boat with him. On the street, men and women stood in pairs and in small groups talking and drinking. Other people jostled along shouting at friends in cafés and laughing at one another. Fernando turned the diamond in his ear. Xury kissed the black man's forehead. I watched the poodle scamper off into the traffic. I thought about Julian unfolding his maps and packing his photograph. I said, "Tell me about the whales, Fernando."

"The big ones can't smell or taste anything."

"Really?"

"And they can't see where they're going or where they've been."

"They're blind?"

"Nope. They have eyes on the side. They can see left and right but not front or back. They can't even see their own flukes. That's how the old-timers would kill them. Row straight at them in a small boat right up to their faces and ram the harpoons deep into their heads."

"And the whales wouldn't know anyone was there?"

"Not unless you made a noise. Whales can hear great."

He told me whales love to be touched and you could drive a dolphin wild just by scratching it with a whisk broom.

I asked Fernando not to walk me to the Harbor Lights. I told him I wanted to think about his whales, their dance, their eyes, his boat, the kids and movie stars and everything.

When I got to the cabin, I sat at the table and stared at the waxing moon through the curtainless window over the sink. The room smelled like the outdoors, salt and pine. I took a good look around for what was ours. I put all my postcards on the table along with the picture of Zoe McDonald and a clutch of folded gas station road maps bound with a thick green rubber band. There it is, I thought. That's us so far. I studied my little pile and realized what Zoe meant, that you could go crazy living the way someone wants you to. Sometimes you have to start trouble. I wrote Julian a note and taped it to the screen door so he couldn't miss it. The note explained how I had decided to stay in Provincetown and how I wanted him to stay with me, but if it came to it, I could always board with Fernando's family or something. I lay down on my bed and waited to hear the scrape of Julian's sandals outside our window.

When I woke, I saw Julian's tie draped over a chair, but no Julian and no note. I found him standing in the water, letting the waves wash over his ankles and shins. I didn't say anything at first. I sat on the cold ground. I thought of all those times we drove through the night. We'd pass these towns on the highway, and I'd say "Tonapah sounds nice," or "Indian Springs probably has hanging gardens." But Julian wouldn't stop. I wanted to see if the towns were as beautiful as their names, but he'd just drive on until morning, and I'd wake up in the back seat, and we'd be in the middle of rocks and sagebrush.

"Come on in, the water's great," Julian said.

"I'm staying."

He nodded. "I got your note."

"So?"

Julian stepped out of the water. "How about some tea?" he said. "I'm shivering."

"Okay, but you won't talk me out of it."

While I brewed the tea, Julian sat at the table and started in about how this was a summer place and wouldn't I like to be down south again for the winter. I remembered what

Fernando had said about the whales. I told Julian he couldn't see where he was going or where he'd been. "You can't even see what's right in front of you."

"What are you talking about?"

I opened the map in front of him and showed him. "Here's Long Beach and here's P-town," I said. "You did it. You got as far away from her as you could."

Julian looked at the map and traced his finger along all the lines of red ink that marked our trip so far. Saw how, for a while there, no matter how far east we'd get, we'd make a loop west again. Eventually, the loops got shorter, like we were escaping the Pacific force field or something. And then after a couple of years we managed to stay east of the Rocky Mountains. Julian smiled. "Jesus, Chloe, maybe you're right."

I told him that Fernando talked to his father and that Mr. Augusto will hire him to work on the *Isabella*, that Mr. Texiera will pay me to clean the bakery on Sunday mornings, that school registration was next Tuesday, and that there were two houses to rent in the West End at off-season rates. "Any other problems?" I said.

Julian didn't look at me. I could hear the waves slap at the rocks and so could he.

"I'll need one of those yellow slickers and some hip boots."

"I adore fishermen," I said.

In the morning I told Fernando the news.

MY LOVE, MY DOVE, MY UNDEFILED

TYLER PATE GIVES the screen door a nudge with his foot, eases it open with his shoulder, and steps out onto the front porch where he sips his black coffee, then sets the cup on the wicker end table. He stretches his arms above his head, yawns, and then retrieves the morning newspaper from beneath the magnolia on the lawn. Tyler sits on the glider, opens the *Clarion,* and first checks the weather forecast—high in the mid-nineties, still no chance of rain—and then his display ad for Pate's Rexall Drugs on page three. Satisfied, Tyler refolds the paper, picks up his coffee cup, and listens to the fading pulse of the tree frogs. It's six A.M., and he has twenty minutes before he makes his four-minute walk to work up Choudrant Street to Broad.

All his life, Tyler Pate has enjoyed just this view of Flandreau, Louisiana, and if much has changed here in forty-two years, this prospect has not: the wisteria-draped picket fence, the cotton fields across the road, once owned by the Pates, now by something called Columbia Chemical, and beyond the fields, the town's water tower, the railroad tracks, and the shotgun houses of the Quarters just now becoming visible in the shrouded light of dawn.

Tyler hears his sixteen-year-old daughter talking on the telephone to her friend Janelle and knows she is wearing the first of several outfits she will try on and then retry on before she needs, finally, to swallow a glass of skim milk, grab a biscuit, and run out to catch the school bus at seven-thirty. Though he cannot make it out just yet, Tyler sees that someone has spray-painted a message on the water tower. This vandalism will give the regulars at the pharmacy's soda fountain something to wag about. Buddy MacDougal will no doubt tell everyone again how it was his boy Lane that painted the Flandreau High School mascot up on that tower in 1965, the year the Flandreau Water Moccasins won the state football championship. Tyler knows it will cost the town eight hundred dollars to hire Caldwell Bryant to paint over the graffiti. Tyler can nearly make it out now. He takes his glasses from his shirt pocket and reads: "Anniece, My Love is Strong as Death."

Tyler calls to his daughter. "Anniece, come out here, please."

Her answer is a melody he's heard a hundred times. "I'm on the phone," she says, drawing the last word out to two syllables.

"Right now, please."

In a minute Anniece stands at the screen door looking out. "What is it, Tyler?"

He wishes she wouldn't call him by his first name. This is a recent affectation of hers, her way, Tyler imagines, of considering him not as her father, nor even as a close relative, but as a fellow resident in this sedate boarding house. He tells her, "Come on outside."

"Okay, I'm out. Now what?"

Tyler points across the road.

"What?"

"Look at the tower, sugar. What do you make of that?"

"Oh, my God! Adlai Birdsong!"

"Say again?"

"The Birdsong boy in my class. He did this."

"Is there something between you and this Adlai Birdsong?"

"Yes, there is," she says. "As much space as possible. Adlai Birdsong is a crazy boy, Tyler. You got to make him stop."

Later that morning Tyler asks his manager, Mavis Willig, to watch the store while he runs a little errand. Yes, he tells her, he'll try to grab a sandwich. Yes, Mavis, it's about the message on the tower, he says. On the walk home to get his car, Tyler notices that the message is done in red paint. He wonders was it love or death that frightened his daughter or was it the way the two came so close together in the same sentence.

The Birdsongs have lived on Avondale Plantation, three miles west of downtown Flandreau, for ten generations. Nearly every black citizen in town is descended from the Avondale slaves except for those who've arrived in recent years and who work at the college over in Grambling. As he drives to Avondale, Tyler recalls his only other visit to the plantation with his daddy in, it must have been, 1954 or 1955, a time when Avondale's descendancy was as yet unpronounced. He recalls the long, winding oyster-shell driveway, the canopy of oaks and pecans, and the grand stucco house with four front doors and a wide, roofed gallery. Young Tyler waited in the idling pickup that time while his daddy took Mr. Travis Birdsong's hepatic medicine to the second of the narrow doors, knocked, bowed slightly, and tipped his hat to the woman who must have answered.

Though no longer prominent and not exactly privileged, the Birdsongs—Royce, Benning, and their boy—are still, if not admired, then respected certainly in Flandreau. The family survives on its history and by leasing out several hundred acres to sharecroppers.

The house is smaller than Tyler expects. The metal roof is badly tarnished and bricks are exposed on the gallery columns. Kudzu has advanced on Avondale from town, but has not yet crossed Bayou Coup de Foudre. When it does, Tyler thinks, there'll be nothing to stop it. It'll sweep through Avondale like wildfire. He parks alongside a brace of camelia bushes, gets out of his car, straightens his tie, and brushes the knees of his slacks. He knocks loudly, one time, at the second of the front doors and waits, knowing that someone will be at home.

"Please, come in, Mr. Pate," the boy says. "Adlai Bird-song, sir. You probably don't remember me from the pharmacy."

Tyler shakes Adlai's hand and steps into what he sees is the kitchen. He sniffs.

"Chicken and dumplings," Adlai says.

"You cook?"

"Yes, sir."

Tyler nods. "I do seem to remember you once in a while buying a cherry Coke, right?"

"And hoping your daughter would come by the store."

"Shouldn't you be in school, Adlai?"

"I should, but mother was ailish this morning." Adlai turns down the flame beneath the dutch oven. "She's better now. Please, come into the parlor, and I'll get my parents."

"Well, actually, since you're home, Adlai, I mean, I'm here to talk about you."

"I know. This way, please."

There are no hallways in this house, a fact which annoys Tyler's sense of order. He likes compartments, likes to be able to put a thing in its place and forget about it, close a door and walk away, to be able to proceed along an uncluttered path without having to step around, as he is doing now in Adlai's wake, the debris of a lifetime.

"Your house is a museum," Tyler says.

"Yes, sir. Father won't allow anything to be thrown out."

In the parlor, Tyler sits on an upholstered divan. Adlai points out the portrait of a Confederate officer with a moonish face, gray whiskers, and a cigar in his left hand. "The gentleman is Colonel Starkey Birdsong. He was killed at Vicksburg. Shot through the eye. And this here is my grandfather Travis Birdsong."

"I remember him. Used to come to the pharmacy quite often."

"I'll get my parents. Excuse me, sir."

Tyler examines the room. On the small oak parlor table beside the divan are someone's collection of silver souvenir spoons, an atomizer, glass figurines, and a metronome. On the mantel over the fieldstone fireplace sit a violin and a bow, a cabinet clock with—Tyler checks his wristwatch—the correct time, and an embossed silver flask. There's a crutch leaning against the mahogany wainscoating in a corner. A black steel safe with gold filagree and a gold dial knob stands beside it. Atop the safe are what look to be an oval, tin, foot tub and a silver chafing dish. Everything in the room is dusted, polished, and useless.

"Pardon us, Mr. Pate. We get so few visitors, you see."

Tyler stands and shakes hands with a man he takes to be his father's age. "Tyler Pate, sir."

"Royce Birdsong, and this is my wife, Mrs. Birdsong. Please, Mr. Pate, sit."

"Thank you."

The Birdsongs are dressed formally, he in a worn, somewhat ill-fitting black tuxedo, she in a lacy, bone-colored evening gown. Royce Birdsong says, "You are whose son, Mr. Pate? Van Buren's?"

"No, sir. Van was my uncle. My daddy's Harrison."

"How is Harrison?"

"Dead, sir. Died two years ago March. Uncle Van, he died it'll be almost five years ago."

"He says the Pate boys are dead," Royce tells his wife who smiles and nods. Royce says he must have known about their passing, now that he thinks about it. "Then you're the boy who married the Turrentine girl from over in Monroe."

"Yes, sir."

"Mrs. Birdsong and I had many lovely times in Monroe, didn't we, dear?" Royce pats the back of his wife's hand as they sit on the couch opposite Tyler. She smiles. "Every year we went to the Mardi Gras Ball at the Layton Castle."

"I know the place."

Mrs. Birdsong, who has in Tyler's mind seemed, until this moment, altogether vacant, says, "Your Anniece is a smart young thing, Mr. Pate."

Tyler is surprised that this porcelain-looking woman has spoken, that she even knows of his daughter's existence, and that knowing of it, thinks admiringly of her. Tyler himself considers Anniece sweet, at least when she is not posing, which lately is all the time. And she's energetic. But he has never thought of her as clever, and neither, he supports himself, have her teachers.

"Why thank you for saying so, Mrs. Birdsong. You've met my daughter then?"

"Oh, no. Adlai tells us all about her though."

"I see. Actually, I've come because of Anniece. My daughter suspects that Adlai here is responsible for a certain message on the water tower."

Adlai, who has been attentively standing in the parlor doorway, says, "Yes, sir, that was me. I love your daughter very much. I want to die with her."

Tyler is struck by the bald intimacy of Adlai's wish. "Adlai," he says, "are you aware that that's a very strange thing to say?"

Adlai looks at his mother. She smiles. "No, sir," he says. "I don't think that."

Tyler is suddenly aware of the closeness of the room, how this two hundred years' accumulation of familial effects seems to be sucking away the air around him. There is an inordinate stillness, he thinks, and a faint aroma of, is it honeysuckle? It's hard for him to think. "Well, Adlai, do you consider this unorthodox method of yours really the best way to win Anniece's affections?"

"I don't know for sure. But I know she won't listen to me when I talk."

"She thinks you're crazy. Why would she think that, Adlai? You're not crazy, are you?"

"Mother says I'm high-keyed."

"That he is, Mr. Pate," Mrs. Birdsong says. "He can be flat rattlebrained on occasion, but he's not crazy. His great-aunt Nopie, she was crazy."

"At least now Anniece knows I love her," Adlai says. "She'll have to talk to me now."

Tyler notices that Mr. Birdsong is asleep. "Adlai, this prank of yours is going to cost the taxpayers eight hundred dollars. There are people in this town who, if they knew who defaced the tower, would want to prosecute."

Mrs. Birdsong tells Tyler what he already knows, that Adlai here is the last Birdsong for now. "Wake your father," she says to Adlai.

Adlai walks over and touches his father's shoulder, and

Mr. Birdsong starts right in on how he met Governor Noe
at one of those Mardi Gras Balls. Tyler checks the time
and says that he must be getting back to work. He says to
Adlai he hopes this nonsense with the tower won't be
repeated.

Mr. Birdsong says, "It looks like we'll be seeing more of
each other, Mr. Pate. I want you to come visit with your
family."

"There's only the pair of us."

"Of course."

"We'll have a garden party," Mrs. Birdsong suggests.
"Get to know each other properly."

"I'll walk you to your car," Adlai says.

Outside the door, he says to Tyler, "So then, she saw
it."

"She did."

"Did she say anything?"

"She did not like it."

"Tell me what I could do to please her."

Tyler opens the car door and looks at Adlai. "I can't tell
you that. I don't know." He shakes his head. "Don't know
what she likes." Tyler understands that this admission is
true and he is surprised.

"I can't hardly sleep," Adlai says. "Every time I do
something, you know, like cooking or like walking in the
fields, I imagine I'm with Anniece and we're talking. We're
laughing or just staring at each other. That's not crazy, is
it?"

"No, it's not."

"I can't even read anymore. I just keep seeing her face."

Adlai shakes his head and smiles. "She must have her mother's eyes."

"Pardon me?"

"Well, sir, your eyes are so dark. You know how Anniece's eyes are that kind of amber."

Tyler's always thought of his daughter's eyes as brown like his own. Mary had blue eyes.

"Is there something she likes? Something I could get for her?"

"Well, let me think."

"I know how much she likes music."

"She does?"

"Oh, yes. She's forever singing."

"You know, Adlai, it might be better if you didn't get her anything just now. Let this message business die down, so to speak."

"I just have to have her, Mr. Pate. I love Anniece."

"Goodbye, Adlai." Tyler shakes his hand.

Tyler is amused to think that his little girl, she of the long faces and the conniption fits, has inspired such ardent desires in anyone, much less in such an unusual and pleasant boy like Adlai Birdsong. Her eyes are amber? Tyler considers that he may not know his daughter as well as even Adlai does. She's vain, he knows that. Or thinks that. She's lovely like her mother was in that restrained and calculated way. What else?

When he drops the car at home, Tyler sees that Caldwell Bryant is up the tower already. Tyler will call Mayor Haley and thank him. Before walking back to the pharmacy, Tyler goes in the house and pours himself a glass of milk. He sits at the kitchen table. Did he ever feel this way, Adlai's way, about any woman? His marriage was warm and decorous enough. He'd met Mary at college in Monroe; they courted loyally, if not passionately. They married after he'd gone to work at his daddy's drugstore, had the baby after waiting long enough to afford the new car, the several insurance policies, and the starter home on Minden Street. Then when Mother died, they all moved to the Choudrant Street house to care for his daddy. And then Mary got cancer, suffered the year of treatments, lost her hair and her weight, screamed at night, and died cursing him for doing this to her.

Marriage did not turn out to be what it could have and should have been. And he lives now with a stranger, his daughter, in this large, austere house, and even she will be leaving him, he knows, at the first opportunity. Did Mary ever love him? Did he love her? They were always considerate, polite to each other. But in love? If it's love that drives you to write on water towers, then no. Neither he nor Mary had ever surprised the other, done anything but the expected. Maybe that's what love is, the unforeseen, not the reliable. His courtship of Mary had been efficiently conducted, cold-blooded, thorough, and successful. No, Tyler's never fallen in love, or whatever it is, in the manner of Adlai Birdsong, and he knows now that he never will.

Suddenly, he is too tired, too spent from the heat, to return to work just yet. He rests his head in his arms and drifts to sleep. He and Adlai are running from the kudzu that pursues them down Broad Street. They are in Confederate uniforms and they turn and follow the railroad tracks. Adlai stumbles. Tyler stoops and asks Adlai, "Why did you pick Anniece to be in love with?"

"Oh, you don't get to choose, Mr. Pate. Not like a horse race. You can't control love."

Tyler lifts Adlai, but the boy has twisted his ankle and needs the crutch. A gust of wind fans the kudzu over the roofs of the houses in the Quarters. "We have to make it to the tower. That's our only chance," Adlai says. But at the tower they are turned back by Caldwell Bryant who tells them there are no more seats. Anniece is up there, they see, and so are Mavis Willig, Kebo Haley, and Lane MacDougal, who died in Vietnam. Royce and Benning are talking to each other and don't hear their names being called.

"Tyler, wake up. Are you sick or something, Tyler?" Anniece shakes her father. "What are you doing home at two-thirty?"

"Two-thirty? No, I'm fine, just tired, I guess. I better get back to the store. Call Mavis, will you, and tell her I'm on my way." Tyler takes a deep breath and rubs his face.

Anniece puts her purse and school books on the table and sits down opposite Tyler. "So?" she says.

"What?"

"Did you take care of it? Adlai Birdsong, I mean."

"I saw Adlai Birdsong this morning. Interesting boy."

"And? So you met him and what?"

"Well, I don't think he'll be writing you any messages soon."

"That's it?"

"I thought that's what you wanted."

"I'm afraid of him, Tyler. He's all the time looking at me."

"He likes you."

"I don't like him."

"Well, I did. I think Adlai's a nice boy. He's smart and serious and polite."

"And totally out of it, and poor as a weevil."

Tyler gets up and goes to the sink. He splashes water on his face and dries it with a paper towel. He looks out the window, sees a mockingbird in the oleander, flashing his wings and fanning his tail. "Why don't you just talk with the boy, Anniece?"

"No."

"Look, you don't need to go out with him. I'm not saying that. But you might like him if you got to know him."

"Adlai Birdsong doesn't figure in my plans."

"He's not in your plans?" Tyler smiles. "Tell me, Anniece, just what plans are these?"

"I'm going to marry someone rich."

"That's a plan?"

"Adlai Birdsong is not rich. Never will be."

"You know, sugar, you don't get to choose who you fall in love with."

"Of course you do. Maybe not in them olden days. But now you do."

Tyler walks to the table, kisses Anniece on the top of her head. "I'm going to work. Can I bring you anything home?"

"Nuh-uh."

"Your eyes are amber."

"I know."

Tyler has to say it. "Don't marry for money. Marry because you love someone."

"And if that someone leaves, dies or something? What then? What am I left with?"

Tyler regards his daughter. "You're too old for your age."

Tyler can't sleep. He's rehearsing a conversation he wants to have with Anniece. A breeze lifts the curtains and rattles the oak outside his bedroom window. We didn't marry for love, your mother and I. We married because we were afraid to be left alone, left behind. Anniece'll catch the irony in that, he thinks. He sees himself and Anniece at Earl K. Long Park watching the wood ducks like they used to do when she was young. He says, your mother and I did the easy thing. Don't blame it on love, what you think happened to me. He tells her that in the end love's all you die with. Well, that and sadness and anger.

Who do you love? he'll ask her. What will she say? I love you, Tyler. She'll say that. And I love Jesus, of course. No, that doesn't count, he'll say. It's too easy. Only love for people counts.

Tyler sees a flash of lightning, counts to himself, and hears the peal of thunder seven miles away. He gets out of bed and closes the window. It's five A.M., and Tyler figures he might as well stay up now. Downstairs, he heats water for coffee. He leans against the sink and wonders if he's ever done anything crazy in his life. So what's crazy, Tyler Pate? Whatever isn't done in Flandreau's crazy. And that covers a wide territory from buying a foreign car or having a cocktail on a Sunday afternoon to going barefoot

on Broad Street. Not so long ago, it was crazy to vote
Republican. And no, Tyler has never done anything crazy.
He wouldn't know how. And here was Adlai Birdsong doing
one mad thing after another just to get Tyler's own self-
involved, stubborn little daughter to speak with him. Tyler
has to smile.

In the month or so since the declaration of love appeared
on the water tower, Adlai has tried several surprising
strategies. One Saturday afternoon he showed up at the
house on his bicycle with a freshly killed chicken, a sack
full of yams, and a tin of rice and spent the day cooking
for Anniece and Tyler while Tyler tried to convince Anniece
to come on down and talk to the boy. When she did finally
leave the room, it was to storm out of the house and walk
to Janelle's where she intended, she said, to sleep over.
    "This is delicious chicken, Adlai."
    "Thank you, sir. Of course, I was hoping Anniece would
get into the spirit of this whirlwind courtship."
    "I understand your disappointment. Pass me the dirty
rice, could you. Thanks."
    "When you cook for someone, that's an act of love, don't
you think?"
    "Yes, I do, Adlai."
Another sultry evening at dusk, Adlai stood in the yard
beneath Anniece's window and played his violin. But not
very well, Tyler thought. Played some sentimental Broad-
way show tunes. Adlai planted a bed of day lillies below
her window, brought her a silver sugar and cream set in a
velvet presentation case. It had been his great-grandmoth-

er's wedding gift to his grandmother and would, his mother said, at last turn Anniece's head. It did not.

"Are you getting discouraged, Adlai?"

"A bit."

"Let's sit on the porch and have us some lemonade."

Tyler filled two tumblers and handed one to Adlai. He sat, looked across at the dusty cotton field and to the water tower shimmering in the afternoon heat, and thought if we don't get some rain soon . . .

"I hope I'm not being a pest, sir."

"You're not." At that moment it seemed crucial to Tyler that he freshen Adlai's flagging spirits. He liked Adlai. He wanted the boy and his dramatic sensibility around. Adlai's pursuit of Anniece had reminded Tyler that there was more to life than the routine of work and home and work again.

Adlai said, "Carrying a football is not an act of love, sir, would you agree?"

"I would."

"So why does Anniece like Riley Whitehead?"

"She does?"

"That's what Janelle tells me."

"Dr. Whitehead's boy?"

"Yes, sir. But he don't know she's alive even."

"Maybe that should make us feel good." Tyler looked at Adlai and smiled. "Maybe not."

Tyler held the tumbler of lemonade to his forehead, then to his cheek. He closed his eyes and tried to picture the girl who had moved to Flandreau from Illinois and sat next to him for a month in ninth grade. What was her name?

"I love Anniece," Adlai said.

"But, Adlai, don't you think you have to know a person first?"

"Yes, sir, I do. I know Anniece. She's not who she wants to be."

"She isn't?"

Adlai shook his head and explained. "She wants to be like the others, but she can't. She pretends that all she cares about are clothes and flirting and stuff."

"Maybe she isn't pretending. Ever think of that?"

"No, I can tell because I watch her. She talks to herself. She bites her bottom lip when she's thinking. What she knows is that she's not like her friends. What she doesn't know is who she really is. That's why she's unhappy. See, she's pretending to be someone else. Of course, if you pretend to be someone else long enough, then you might as well be someone else."

"Well, don't be discouraged now, Adlai."

"I'll try not to, but even a crazy boy will slam his head on a steel door only so long."

Tyler laughed at that. "So," he said, "you admit you're crazy."

"Crazy in love."

Tyler sipped his lemonade and looked across to the water tower and then at Adlai on the glider beside him. "You think she's afraid?"

"Yes. Afraid of me and of what people might think. Afraid of herself. That's why she won't talk to me. She might hear that she's not who she thinks she is."

"Adlai, you're a smart boy."

"I'm smart about Anniece. That's about it."

"You think she's afraid of talking to you because if she likes you, that would ruin her rich-husband fantasy?"

"I don't know, but if she winds up with someone who doesn't realize how afraid she is, who doesn't know that she doesn't know she's afraid, well, she'll be scared for the rest of her life."

"That would be regrettable."

"If she would just talk to me I could help her see what's so interesting, so likable about herself. She'd be happy and so would I. I could even settle for being her brother," Adlai said. "At least for a while."

Tyler takes his cup of coffee to the front porch to watch the storm approach from the west. Five miles away now. He wonders what will happen to him? Unlike the Birdsongs who stay in the house after they die, the Pates vanish, their lives having none of those vivid details that a memory can latch on to. He'll end up, he knows, alone in this empty house on Choudrant Street in Flandreau, Louisiana. He'll have less and less to say to folks. Mavis Willig will pass on; a discount drug store chain will open a branch and Pate's Rexall will close, and he'll wind up sitting here on this porch staring at the water tower. Anniece will live in New Orleans with the doctor she'll meet at LSU. She'll invite him down to visit at Christmas and Mardi Gras, but he won't go. When he gets sick, she'll shift him to a nursing home, sell the house, get on back to her charity work in the city.

The tower looks imposing in the flash of lightning. Three miles away. The air turns cool. Adlai Birdsong hasn't been by in two weeks. He has given up on Anniece, it seems. Won't people be surprised if old Tyler Pate just one day up and leaves town without a fare-thee-well? Tyler smiles. They go to pick up their hair tonic and valium, but the store is dark. I guess we really didn't know the guy that well, someone like Buddy MacDougal will say. Go figure. He must have had people elsewhere. Yes, sir, must have gone to his people.

Tyler can make out the wisteria shaking on the fence as the wind tries to blow it free. In the stroke of lightning, he sees the blooming, thirsty cotton like a field of snow. The heat has lifted. It's raining, thundering. Tyler steps off the porch and lets the drops drill his head and face. He can see in the lightning that there is a new message on the tower. "My . . . my sister," it says. "My sister, my love," and something else. He waits for the lightning. "My dove, my un-de-filed."

"Tyler, what are you doing?" Anniece, in her robe, is standing on the porch, hollering to her father.

"Look," he points to the tower.

"Come out of the rain."

"I can't," he says, and "Look at the tower. It's for you."

Anniece squints. "What's it say?"

Tyler yells above the thunder, "My sister, my love, my dove, my undefiled."

She shakes her head.

"Adlai's back. What do you think of that?"

"He's crazy."

"Yes. I'd better have a talk with him. I'll see you later."

"Tyler, you get up here this minute. You'll catch your death."

"But, sugar this is the first rain in seven weeks."

"What if someone sees you? They'll think you're a lunatic. Now, come on."

"Make me."

"What?"

"Come and fetch me back."

Anniece walks out on the steps, and the rain flattens the hair onto her forehead. She cringes and closes her eyes. But then she looks at Tyler, at the pajamas clinging to his legs and his thin white chest and the hair all plastered to his head like he'd been licked by a large cat. And she laughs. And Tyler laughs with her and thinks about this rain, the storm, and how you never expect the world to look like this, dark and light at the same time.

THE SLOW DEATH OF THE B MOVIE

"THESE MOVIES ARE a perilous business," my grand-father said. "Just look at what happened to Mr. Dillin-ger—had to see a movie so bad he got hisself blown to Kingdom Come at the Biograph Theatre. What kind of art is that that drives a sane man to lunacy?" He wasn't expecting an answer, my grandfather. He was simply "dis-coursing," as he called it. We were on hands and knees cleaning the marble floor in the lobby of the Washburn Building, me with a putty knife, my grandfather, a wire brush. This was our usual Sunday afternoon those days in

Worcester, Massachusetts, the Heart of the Common-
wealth.

He took a last drag and flipped his cigarette into the
bucket of sudsy ammonia and water. "And what about us,
Johnny? Sure we're taking the Devil's own chance down
at the Rialto." He slugged a gulp of wine, screwed on the
cap, and replaced the flat bottle in his hip pocket. "Our
sense of reality is being hammered to smithereens one reel
at a time."

"That's the last of the gum," I said, wiping the putty
knife on the thigh of my dungarees.

"We're being seduced by illusion. You know that, don't
you, Johnny? We've got to face facts."

"I'll just rinse and we're finished."

"Wonderful! Then we'll go to the movies."

The Rialto Theatre stood two blocks from the Common
in the direction of the now abandoned Union Train Sta-
tion. Beside the Rialto was the cast-iron Washburn Build-
ing, where my grandfather, Eamon Fitzmichael, and I lived.
This entire block from the Greyhound Bus Terminal to
Palace Billiards was leveled in the early sixties to make
way for a downtown shopping mall.

Eamon and I occupied two rooms on the second floor
of the Washburn in what had been the offices of Nuclear
Family, a bankrupt construction firm that had designed
and built backyard fallout shelters. Eamon was the build-
ing's custodian, and in those pre-demolition days of the
late fifties, his job was relatively easy, there being only four
remaining tenants on all three floors.

Konrad Wondolowski III was the CPA and Notary Pub-
lic in Room 321. He had eyes like blue ice. He was tall,

over six feet, thin and round-shouldered. Konrad III generally slept at his desk every afternoon, but would awaken immediately upon hearing the rackety cage door of the elevator slide open. His only customers were our other tenants.

Dewey Cature, a wiry sixty-year-old with a shock of milk-white hair and horn-rim glasses with half-inch-thick lenses, insisted that he was the deceased Henry Ford. In fact, Dewey always introduced himself as "Dewey-Cature-the-late-Henry-Ford" as if it were all one word. Dewey was trying to get his automobile company back from the "blackguards who stole it from me." The litigation required reams of affidavits, briefs, and torts, none of which Dewey would entrust to a lawyer, so every page was notarized by Konrad III. Dewey had the legend "Ford Motor Car Company, Temporary World Headquarters" stenciled on the pebbled glass of his office door.

Dewey didn't get along with Clifford King, the inventor (Edison Again, Inc.) on the top floor. Dewey thought Clifford would blow up the building and incinerate his valuable legal documents one of these days. Dewey also told me privately one morning that he had good reason to believe that Clifford was working for the "other side."

"The Russians, Dewey?"

"Venusians."

Actually, Clifford managed to market at least two of his inventions that I know of. He patented thimbles of oilcloth that fit over your fingers for eating lobster and this kind of tape with two sticky sides that you put on the bottom of your boots in icy weather. He had other ideas, too, like a wireless TV so thin you could frame it and hang it on the wall like a Picasso, but as far as I know, they never made it beyond the third floor of the Washburn.

The fourth tenant was Eamon's chief means of support. Chickie Dipasquale took bets on athletic and political events and ran the downtown numbers pool. He kept Konrad III afloat by having him notarize a flood of IOUs and kept Eamon busy collecting bets and running to Weintraub's deli for tripe-and-egg specials.

Several evenings a month, Eamon would pop over to Lucky Liquor and pick up a fifth of something like Tawny Port, and we would walk next door to the Rialto, where the marquee always read, "Fifteen Cents. Lowest Adm. in T wn."

The Rialto was dying the same slow death as the B movies it featured. A crack in the ticket-booth window was mended with duct tape; the wooden seats were splintered, many were armless; the maroon stage curtain was faded in long pink streaks, and the screen itself was torn in the shape of a smile in the lower left-hand corner. The Rialto ran continuous shows twenty-four hours a day. Every performance included a Pathé newsreel, a cartoon (usually black-and-white and always teeming with frenetic little mice), and two features. Eamon enjoyed the newsreels because they included highlights from the latest championship prizefight. We saw Sugar Ray Robinson KO Bobo Olson in two rounds on the same bill with *Creature with the Atom Brain* and *Them*. If we saw the newsreel first, Eamon would be asleep midway through the first feature unless it was one of those Abbott-and-Costello-Meet-Somebody screwball horror flicks. He loved those.

The Rialto's feature fare ran to recirculated Monogram

and Republic low-budget films and recently released science-fiction thrillers, which were all the rage then. The actors were always pleasant to look at, and the plots were unencumbered with significance. I loved them all. I watched so many atomic-mutant horror movies that I imagined Richard Denning was my unknown father, and I dreamed of growing up to be a university scientist with a convertible, a loyal and lovely lab assistant, and a destiny to save the world from alien invaders. (And that's why I went to school regularly and hated when Eamon was hungover and I had to stay home to mind him and the Washburn. That's why I was adored by the nuns at St. Stephen's Grammar School. I was an aggressive, if not always brilliant, student spurred on by my dreams of walking through the Mojave moonlight with Evelyn Ankers and telling Lyle Talbot when to fire the flamethrowers: "Not yet, General. Wait till you see the green of their antennae.")

There were those inspirational youth movies featuring star quarterbacks at good old State U who looked thirty years old, fell in love with shiny little coeds, and hoped their fathers would live long enough to hear the broadcast of the big Navy game this Saturday. And there were the nightclub movies.

Kitty, a star-struck clerk at Macy's, meets a charming gangster who buys a failing Italian restaurant and turns it into the hottest club on Broadway, and now he wants her to be the headline singer at the Flamingo. "Oh, Jimmy!" she says with her arms around his neck. He blushes and sends her to Gimbels with the boys to buy a splashy new wardrobe. "And see that she's at the club by six," he tells the boys. "Sure, Boss," they say. "Come on, Miss Drake."

All the while, we realize that shortly the law, or some rival gangster, will begin to put the squeeze on Jimmy and that thirty-five minutes into the movie Kitty will fall for a dapper young law student—maybe he's even Jimmy's kid brother whom Jimmy promised his dying mother he'd always look out for.

Nightclubs flourished in those midcentury epics. Even Roy Rogers, fresh from bustin' broncos and corralling cattle rustlers in some time-warped Western town, would end up with the Sons of the Pioneers wowing the sophisticates in New York with his bangled buckskin shirts and his cornball cowboy lyrics in some cavernous club along the Great White Way.

Picture Jimmy's Flamingo: lean women in slinky black evening gowns and gloriously upswept hairdos sip gimlets and laugh carelessly with fawning, tuxedoed gents who finger their mustaches as the sixty-piece orchestra, all musicians identically blazered and coiffed, swings through "Sentimental Journey." The chandeliers shimmer in the polish of the dazzling dance floor. You make your entrance. You call the doorman Tommy and tip him indulgently. You harbor a secret lust for this adorable hat-check girl but know it will never work. The maître d' holds your table and admires your insistence on a cheery little Beaujolais. You buy your Pall Malls from the cigarette girl in the cheerleader outfit and the bellhop's cap. Your waiter, a swarthy sort with an undefinable accent, lights your smoke. And everyone around you is so swell, so suave, so splendid.

There, at the next table, a sensitive and serious university science professor. He's perhaps slightly uncomfortable out of his academic environment. He fidgets a bit, pushes the glasses up on his nose. Coughs. And yet is still able to enjoy the company of his lovely lab assistant, the adoring Marlene, daughter of the venerable department chairman. He might even ask her to dance. Yes, she might like that. He *will* ask her to dance.

And then the screen goes white, the film ticks in the projector, and the lights come up. I nudge Eamon awake. "Did we repel the aliens?" he wants to know. I longed for that urbane Gotham way of life that I watched in the dark at the Rialto. One night, I peeked through the alley window of the El Rocco Room behind the Washburn hoping to catch a glimpse of forty chorus girls with cardboard violins tap-dancing their hearts out in the spotlight. But all I saw in that dark and smoky bar was the tops of oiled pompadours and revolving Rheingold beer signs. I was disappointed and confused, but I figured everything would be copacetic after I finished college on a football scholarship, got my driver's license, turned twenty-one, and accumulated the sufficient discretionary income to manage a George Sanders kind of life-style.

About the time I discovered that a university scientist would need at least a casual acquaintance with math and that singing cowboys were never tone-deaf, the Washburn tenants were notified by registered letter that our building was to be razed. That was the summer of 1961. I was thirteen, and the Rialto had closed for ostensible renovation the previous Christmas. I wondered what my grandfather and I would do. Homelessness was just the sort of situation that might draw the attention of the Welfare. Then I'd have to watch some caseworker chew his eraser, put down the pencil, and wonder, well, just where's the rest of your family, son? and so on. All the rest there ever was was my mom, who worked at the junior high cafeteria and made the money the three of us lived on. She was a silent woman who slept on the parlor couch near the radio. One day she told Eamon, "Da, I'm going to the five-and-dime for nail-polish remover," and that was the last of mother. Left town with a school janitor. He was married. I was six.

Thayer Realty, owners of the Washburn and much of the rest of downtown Worcester, told Eamon they were sorry, but they had no janitorial openings. It was unlikely that anyone else would hire a sixty-seven-year-old alcoholic even if he could varnish woodwork like nobody's business. In the movies, a righteous citizens' group would rise up and block the demolition, citing the historic value of the Washburn, its irreplaceable architectural integrity, and Eamon would make an impassioned speech in the City Council chambers, become a folk hero, and so on.

What happened instead was that we had a farewell party on the day that Chickie and Konrad III closed their offices. We still had thirty days before the city workers arrived to board the windows and rip out the copper pipes. Chickie's wife, Tillie, arrived with a tray of cannolis and anise cookies. Chickie had two gallons of Vino Fino and a quart of Moxie delivered from Lucky Liquor. We set up our refreshments on the old maple church pew in the Ford Motor Car Company's Temporary World Headquarters. Dewey passed around the dessert tray. Clifford said he couldn't possibly eat. He didn't know how he was ever going to move thirty-two years' worth of notes, charts, drawings, pamphlets, burners, beakers, cabinets, meters, scales, tables, drills, clamps, screws, and toggle bolts. Dewey suggested that he invent an antigravity machine and float the whole mess to the city dump.

Konrad III had no such logistical problem. He was locking his door this afternoon and letting the inevitable steel ball bury his paperwork. He was moving to White River Junction to live with his three older sisters in a small flat over a candy store, and he had the train ticket in his vest pocket. Konrad III strapped on his accordion, closed his eyes, and played the "Auld Lang Syne Polka."

Dewey insisted the impostors at Ford were behind the eviction. They had stolen his company and now were hounding him from his office-in-exile. It was unfortunate, he said, that the rest of us had become victims of the vendetta. Chickie said it wasn't the Ford Motor Company at all; it was just progress.

Eamon sat quietly on an examination table picking at the foam beneath the cracked Naugahyde and sipping wine from a paper cup. He told Tillie that he and I would do okay. We were like Abbott and Costello, he said. We'd muddle our way through somehow. Maybe we'd move to Hollywood where it's always warm and your breakfast grows on trees. Maybe we'd sell bowlers for the Susquehanna Hat Company. Tillie smiled at me. She said, "Chickie, it's time to leave."

Chickie offered Konrad III a lift to the station and Clifford a ride home. So we all said our goodbyes at the ele-

vator door. Before he left, Konrad III handed his notary
stamp to Dewey and winked. "You must know my signa-
ture by now."

I helped Dewey take down the photos of Edsels from
his office walls. Eamon, now lying on the table, said he'd
be glad to help except that his arm hurt. "Good thing it's
not my drinking arm," he joked. Dewey promised as soon
as he got this little legal matter cleared up, we'd all be
sunning ourselves on the beach in Detroit. "My arm hurts
real bad," Eamon said. Dewey called an ambulance.

Eamon had a stroke. He spent his first week at City Hos-
pital in a windowless ward with eleven other patients and
two empty beds. I was disappointed that none of the nurses
were as comely, crisp, and wholesome as those who cared
for Ronnie Reagan and the obligatory Italian kid from
Brooklyn who would be dead before the movie ended. The
stroke had weakened Eamon's left arm, gimped his left leg,
and clouded his mind. Each morning at eight-thirty, Dewey
came to the Washburn and walked me to the hospital.

Chickie and Tillie kept me in food and pocket money
and wanted me to move in with them until Eamon came
home. I liked them enough, but I was afraid of their sons,
these large football-playing twins who whispered about me
when they visited the Washburn. They thought Marvel
comic books were interesting. They told me that Jerry Lewis
was funny. I figured I had a better chance of surviving my
new social worker, whose bright idea was to place me in a
foster home. Clifford called the Welfare, said he was my
uncle and that he and his mother were caring for me. That
gave the social worker the excuse to move on to more urgent
cases.

Living alone was not the adventure I'd hoped it would
be. I wanted a gang of pals like Leo Gorcy had in *Pride of
the Bowery*, guys you could joke and scheme with, guys
with names like Diesel, Dog, Rip, and Mickey. I imagined
us beating the rich kids from the West Side in absolutely
every sport and then helping the cops solve a series of baf-
fling burglaries in Chinatown. But I had no friends. I didn't
even have a cat, a horse, or a cozy corner of the bunk-
house, just two rooms in the Washburn, and those for only
seventeen more days.

I never turned the lights on. Nights I sat in the comfort-
able Rialto-like dark and stared out of my window at the
people on Front Street, sometimes until I could hear the
grackles screeching awake in the elms on the Common.
After midnight most people ambled along alone as if the
street itself were the destination. The Greyhound Termi-
nal was open all night and men gathered like moths in its
lighted doorway. A woman in a white dress and white
loafers stops at the taxi stand and shifts her weight from
leg to leg. A brown leather purse is slung over her right
shoulder and a blue jacket is draped over her left arm. She
holds a paper bag in both hands. She's a waitress going
home, I figure, with leftover raviolis. She'll warm the sauce
on the stove and eat off a TV tray and watch the Late
Show. Then she'll kick off her shoes and rub her aching
feet. She'll lean back on the couch, light a cigarette, and
stare at the water spot on the ceiling. She'll think about
what it would be like to live in California. She'll want to
tell someone about her lousy day at the restaurant. Some-
times I wanted to talk to the people I watched.

A few days after Eamon's second minor stroke, the hospital transferred him to a nursing home. I took that as a promising sign—the next logical move would be to the Washburn. Never happen in two weeks, Dewey said. He didn't like it. "That's where they send a person who can't take care of himself anymore," he told me. "But he doesn't have to take care of himself" is what I would have told the doctors if they had asked.

The first morning Dewey and I visited the Houghton Manor Nursing Home, we found Eamon alert and feisty but looking like someone else. We sat in the solarium with a handful of other patients, two of whom rocked themselves rhythmically in their wheelchairs while a third pretended to shampoo his hair at an imaginary basin. "Cripes, the place is full of loonies," Eamon said out loud, just like that, but nobody reacted. Eamon was pajamaed and robed. He'd been given a disturbing haircut, one that an Eastern European refugee in a British melodrama would have. His fingernails had somehow thickened and curved like talons. White hairs grew from his nose and ears. He told us he had rifled a number of bureaus and closets in patients' rooms the night before and had come up with a fifth of Wild Irish Rose. I said, "Suppose you had gotten caught?" He said, "They're so doped up, this crew, they sleep like babies." I said it still wasn't right.

No one would tell Eamon when he'd be released. Dewey suspected they'd be watching Eamon like hawks, waiting for an excuse to pump him with drugs or worse. I said, "Come on, Dewey, they'll see he's okay, just doesn't move so gracefully anymore and maybe he forgets a bit, that's all." But that wasn't all. Eamon continued his nightly raids and wound up getting caught three times by the same nurse, not with contraband liquor, but with clothing. He'd duck into a sleeping patient's room, open the closet door, snap on the light, and if he saw a shirt he liked, he'd put it on. Shirts, hats, pants, anything. It wasn't exactly stealing, he said, because he was replacing the pilfered clothes with his own. And anyway, can't they take a joke, he said. The nurse, a 250-pound guy named Rizzuti, was not amused. "What's a man want to be a nurse for anyway?" Eamon complained. That's not the point, we tried to tell him. "You have to be on your best behavior or you'll never get out of here."

Incarceration took its toll. Eamon's behavior grew more unpredictable. We never knew how we'd find him. One afternoon he played all the Irish tunes he knew on the green piano in the lobby and had the staff and patients singing and clapping along. A man in blue pajamas danced a reel. "I should have been a nightclub singer," Eamon joked. "They love me, don't they, Johnny?"

But the next morning he wouldn't talk except to accuse us of double-crossing him, and we knew damn well what he meant, so don't play dumb with him, he said.

"What are you talking about?" I said.

"You put me in here, didn't you?"

"No, I didn't. You're sick."

He laughed at me.

I said, "Why won't you get better?"

He said, "Why don't you get lost!"

I cried and Eamon told Dewey to get the crybaby out of his sight. As we stood to go, Eamon looked at the ceiling and said, "Well, aren't you your mother's boy-o, walking out on me like this."

On the way home, Dewey bought me a vanilla Coke at
the bus terminal and blamed Eamon's behavior on the
drugs they must be filling him with. All I could think about
was what would happen in nine days when the Washburn
closed for good. If Eamon did not get better, what would
they do with me?

"We'll have to break him out of here. That's all there is
to it."

"What, Dewey?"

"Drink up, my boy. We have plans to make."

First we neutralize the enormous nurse. We divert his
attention. Then we enter Eamon's room, wake him, dress
him, and whisk him out the back to an awaiting getaway
Ford. Finally, we speed off to Detroit or some other time-
warped Western town. Sounded foolproof to me. Dewey
suggested several elaborations to heighten the sense of
adventure, you know, like dressing in black, coasting down
the drive with the headlights out, that sort of thing.

When we whispered the plan to him, Eamon whispered
back that it had taken us long enough to come up with it.
Did we think he was Superman or something? He said
they were giving him truth pills at night. They were after
information, he said, but he was too strong for them. He
had us follow him to his room and then shut the door.
After a check of the closet, Eamon pulled a postcard of
the Old Man of the Mountain from his pillowcase and
handed it to me. "This is the kind of thing I have to put
up with."

I told him it was a get-well note from Konrad III.

"Konrad III? What is he? The King of Poland?"

"You know Konrad III. Wondolowski. The notary public."

"Notary public, my eye."

We told Eamon we'd be back for him Friday at midnight. In the meantime, Dewey said, we'd be lying low. Eamon said he'd be waiting; he'd be acting natural so as not to attract attention.

Clifford gave us a glass cutter and a plunger to get us through Eamon's window. The sulfur bombs would presumably occupy the nurse, and the lobster finger bibs would cover our prints. We promised Clifford we'd write from Michigan and drove off in Dewey's rented Falcon. Dewey said we should probably have a code name for our mission, and we came up with Operation Manorbreak. Sounded enough like an Audie Murphy movie to me. So here we were, a couple of desperadoes about to pull off a dazzling caper right under the noses of the big boys. By the time they noticed anything missing, we'd be over the state line driving into the sunset. This was definitely better than walking out the front door in broad daylight.

Eamon wouldn't be 100 percent. I knew that. Probably never would be, but he'd be better off with us in Detroit than in the nursing home. I knew that, too. Then I wondered if he might have been faking this eccentric behavior to make us feel so guilty and rotten that we'd break him out. Or what if this was all a test? Say Clifford and Dewey and everyone were in on it. To see if I had the courage to rescue my grandfather from the jaws of death, so to speak. That was the plot of *The Metalunan Virus*, which I had seen four times. Whatever the case, one thing was certain—Eamon and I would be together in minutes. It was eleven fifty-eight P.M.

Our movie took a comic turn. Dewey brandished the glass cutter like a stiletto, but its tiny wheel just rolled along the screen. The sulfur bombs might have been successfully distracting if we had remembered the matches. Dewey hustled back to the idling car for his notary stamp, which we used to hammer out the base of the screen. No sign of the nurse. I whispered Eamon's name into the darkness of the room, then boosted myself through the window, eased myself to the floor, and crawled to the bed. It was empty.

The door opened, and in the backlight from the hall, I recognized my grandfather. When he snapped on the overhead light, I saw what he had evidently meant by "acting natural." He wore baggy red Bermuda shorts that reached below his knees, white gloves, and a sleeveless Pat Boone cardigan. No chance he'd attract attention like that.

"Let's go," I said. "Come on, Dewey's waiting in the car."

Eamon answered me slowly, looking at his gloves the whole time. He said, "I thought I told you loonies to stay out of my room."

I told him to cut the comedy, we had to get out pronto. "You're a free man, Eamon."

"I said if you came back here I'd have to muckle you, now didn't I?"

I said, "Eamon, it's me, " and I grabbed his left hand to lead him to the window. He slapped me across the face with his right. It was the first time I'd ever been hit, and it hurt like mad. I tried to say, "What are you, crazy or something?" but choked on the words. Then the nurse was at the door. Eamon said, "Rizzuti, get him out of my house!" And the nurse said, "He doesn't know you anymore, son. You should leave now."

I sat in the kitchen of my foster parents' home and studied the architect's sketch of the new mall which the newspaper hailed as the salvation of a dying city—all right angles, plate glass, and concrete, not lovely, but then redemption doesn't have to be, I figured. "Demolition Slated for Washburn Block," read the headline. I noted the date. I lived with the Sullivans in four rooms over Stirling's five-and-dime. Dave was a mailman, Kath a clerk at Gannon's Bakery. They had lost their son in Korea. They were kind and loved me as well as they could. We went to church and restaurants together. I could sit on the bed in my own room, watch the traffic on Grafton Street, and think about Eamon. Except that every time I did I saw that lunatic Eamon who had menaced and abandoned me. I couldn't struggle past this counterfeit to the man who loved newsreels.

The first Monday in February I skipped school to watch them raze the old Rialto. I met Dewey outside the boarded-up Greyhound station. A photographer in a tweed overcoat snapped pictures as the wrecker's ball tore through the marquee. Dewey pulled his scarf over his nose and stamped his feet against the cold. I told him how Eamon thought the movies were dangerous stuff. I told him about

John Dillinger. He told me Dillinger was shot outside the Biograph, not in the theater. It's leaving the movies that'll kill you, he said. Know what I mean?

In the movies, the juvenile lead would have steeled his nerves and returned to Houghton Manor with religious regularity, and through the force of his will and the goodness of his heart, would have led his grandfather back to sanity and health. And all would live happily . . . and other illusions. What happened though was I never visited my grandfather again in the year that he lived. So when Sister Superior called me out of class one afternoon to tell me that he had passed away, I felt shame and relief. The man in the red Bermuda shorts had finally died. Sister told me to pray. I closed my eyes and imagined Eamon and there he was, slumped in his seat, stinking of that sweet wine, beside me again in the dark at the Rialto. I tell him, yes, we zapped the alien, and he winks at me. And I said, yes, Sister, I'd like to lie down in the infirmary. I want to think about this. Thank you, Sister. Yes.

THE FONTANA GENE

WHEN BILLY WAYNE Fontana's second wife, Tami Lynne, left him for the first time, he walked into Booker T. Washington Elementary School, interrupted the fourth grade in the midst of a hygiene lesson, it being a Thursday morning and all, apologized to Miss Azzie Lee Oglesbee, the substitute teacher, fetched his older boy, Duane, and vanished for a year and a half from Monroe. Tami Lynne remarked how spiteful it was of Billy Wayne to take just the one child and not the other. "He's always been partial to Duane," she told a reporter from the *Citizen*, "and it just breaks my heart." She patted her little harelipped six-year-old on his head. "Poor little Moon Pie," she said.

Channel 10 has this part of the news called Crime Stoppers where our Sheriff's Department acts out some unsolved crime or other and asks you, the viewing audience, to call this one special number should you have a lead of any kind which might result in the apprehension and/or conviction of the alleged perpetrators. So one night they perform the "Billy Wayne Kidnapping," which is what they were calling it then, and Sheriff Buddy Tidwell himself plays Billy Wayne and Buddy's boy Boogie plays Duane. They get one call on the special number and it's from Steve Yarborough over at You-All Rental, the guy with the hairline mustache and sorghum voice you see all the time on the cable TV commercials. Steve Yarborough says that Billy Wayne did come by on the afternoon in question, rented a cap for his pickup and two very expensive down sleeping bags. So Buddy tells him you best call your insurance company in the morning. Might as well tell you now that Steve Yarborough's insurance agent is Billy Wayne's first wife, Earlene. That's the kind of town Monroe is.

To be honest, we were not at all surprised at this episode nor at the calamities which ensued. The fact is that the Fontana family has had an illustrious history of catastrophe in our parish. They have what folks used to call a curse, but now we know better. What the Fontanas have is bad water in the gene pool.

Around 1840, the first known Fontana sloshed his way out of the spongy gumbo of the Delta somewhere between here and Vicksburg. Rose up out of that sticky, primordial ooze, one person said, like sin percolating up through the slime of your subconscious. Madison Tensas, in his antebellum history of northeast Louisiana, mentions this first Fontana, who stunk like marsh gas, had webbed fingers, and caused a panic among the women and children of Talla Bena when he appeared on Main Street in nothing but alligator-hide drawers. This was Peregrine Fontana, who sired twin albino sons before he was drowned in Bayou Macon by capricious foot soldiers under the command of General Grant.

Mangham and Bosco Fontana and their several wives, dozen children, converts, and hired hands wandered the Delta for forty years claiming to be the Lost Tribe of Israel. They made a living fishing, trapping, and selling acres of swampland that they did not own to freed slaves and the occasional carpetbagger. About the time that the effects of Reconstruction had mitigated, a time when everyone found, or was led to, his rightful niche in the new society, the Fontanas appeared at the banks of the Ouachita River at a marshy clearing just north of Monroe called Chauvin Bottom, claimed it was their Promised Land, and settled in for good and all. That's when our great-grandfathers first noticed that all of the Fontana children were male and dispatched a worried delegation of ministers and physicians to investigate. Some of the gentlemen who gathered daily at the Biedenharn Pharmacy for phosphates and dominoes considered the Fontana reproductive anomaly to be a most propitious phenomenon and wondered if it might not be a matter of some easily learned technique. Other folks, however, thought the circumstances peculiar at best, while one or two whispered their suspicions of infanticide. But that was not the case. It was a simple, if ineffable, manifestation of the Lord's will, the delegation concluded. Perhaps that is God's only way of keeping the Fontana men from committing the abominable sin of incest, they went on.

In addition to being the most executed white family in the history of Louisiana (twelve Fontanas, starting with Bosco's oldest boys, Jupiter and Saturn, in 1909 and ending with Desoto in 1935, where hanged for crimes against property), the Fontanas have also been the sickest. In 1914, influenza swept Chauvin Bottom, a full four years before the pandemic that followed the Great War, and reduced the Fontana population by two-thirds. Then came yellow fever, an outbreak of encephalitis, a mysterious case of leprosy, and a legion of consumptives. Now all of this time, the Fontanas were keeping pretty much to themselves except for the yearly cane harvests, and the townsfolk, though periodically apprehensive, were quite content to stay their distance.

Thirty-two Fontanas survived the flood of 1927—this was before the levee, now. Among them was a youngish woman so debilitated, so haggard and brittle that she was hurried directly to St. Francis Hospital over the muttered objections of her clan. Tests sure enough proved that Aphrodite Fontana was both profoundly syphilitic and seven months pregnant. On that Fourth of July, a day so unbearably hot that water moccasins dropped from the trees into Bayou DeSiard, a day still remembered by our old-timers as the day it rained snakes, on that Independence Day,

Positive Wassermann Fontana was born blind, feeble-minded, and otherwise congenitally cursed. Aphrodite was not so lucky. She did not survive the birth.

Nor did doctors expect "Little Pee Dubya," as he came to be compassionately nicknamed, to live much beyond his first weeks, given the nutritional and environmental hardships he was certain to encounter there with his family back in the Bottom. One of our professors at the state college first speculated that perhaps a kind of reverse Darwinism was at work among the Fontanas and that somehow "survival of the sorriest" was the rule. And then wouldn't you know along comes the war to hurry the devolution along. All the world's able-bodied men go out and murder each other and you even begin to think the professor's not just talking about the Fontanas. At any rate, by 1943, Positive Wassermann is the only living male Fontana, the only carrier of the inherited material therefore, and the town dared to think that at last the durable Fontana chromosome had played itself out. But Positive Wassermann lived thirty-one years and begat a son and called him Billy Wayne. And all the days of Positive Wassermann were thirty-three years, and he died ingloriously enough in Monroe's Mental Jail. Billy Wayne's mother, a defective child of thirteen, unable to care for her baby or even to comprehend their relationship, was shunted off to a juvenile facility in West Carroll Parish.

The Fontana tribe, reduced to its women, converts, and assorted hangers-on, and deprived of even the dubious leadership of Positive Wassermann, drifted quietly and mysteriously away from Chauvin Bottom and Monroe. One morning that fall, when the fog had lifted, all that remained of the Fontana camp was the smoldering ashes of the fire in which they had burned everything they could not carry, everything except a leatherette Recline-o-Chair which had served as Positive Wassermann's throne and now sat in a puddle of green water beneath a withered live oak. The infant Billy Wayne, the only descendent of Peregrine Fontana and tabernacle of his formidable gene, was abandoned to the care of the good Sisters of St. Francis, who, with the unspoken complicity of the town, devised and executed a strategy to rid the world for good and all of the Fontana aberration, a solution at once so inspired and so diabolical it could only have originated, our Pentecostals believed, with the Pope of Rome himself. Billy Wayne was to be groomed for the priesthood.

Little Billy Wayne grew up in the convent wing of the hospital, coddled by his twenty-one wimpled maiden aunts, and trained in theology by Monsignor Pargoud, the hospital chaplain. Billy Wayne spoke Latin before Southern, a circumstance so peculiar that he was put on Art Baker's *You Asked for It* television program and driven down to Baton Rouge to meet Governor Jimmie Davis, the singer and actor. For his part, Billy Wayne was an enthusiastic student and was often heard memorizing his Baltimore Catechism in the shade of the convent's grape arbor. He took to wearing his altar-boy cassock regularly, even in the extreme heat of summer, and even on outings to Forsythe Park, which set him distinctly apart from other children.

It is probably unwise, unhealthy even, for a child who has yet to reach the age of reason to entertain notions of martyrdom and sacrifice. Consider what profound disappointment must await the boy who understands himself to be a tool for the salvation of others. We must be mindful, however, that Billy Wayne grew up riding his three-wheeler along the tiled corridors of the chronic wards and so was early on exposed to the unlovely countenance of the human condition. Perhaps it is natural that an impressionable child who constantly wanders through a cloud of loss will confuse the ignominy of illness with the nobility of suffering.

When he turned thirteen, Billy Wayne was sent to a Dominican novitiate up north in Kentucky or thereabouts. In seven years he figured to be ordained a priest, to take the solemn vows of poverty, obedience, and chastity. We held our breaths and prayed for Billy Wayne. He had been called to God, so he said, to serve the sick, and he proposed to spend his life in service to the lepers at the hospital in Carville. And he would begin his training that first summer vacation ministering to the sick right here at St. Francis.

While other fourteen-year-old boys played Dixie League baseball or maybe worked trotlines on the bayou, Billy Wayne performed the Corporal Works of Mercy at the hospital, visiting the conscious, feeding the week, bathing the sores of the terminal. You're going to make a fine priest, a holy priest, aren't you, Billy Wayne? we'd say to him. After Billy Wayne had brought Lanny Johns back to life, Monsignor Pargoud wrote the bishop in Alexandria and told him how Mr. Johns's heart monitor and the other machines had all gone quiet, and how the duty nurse was already on the phone to Poteet Funeral Home, and how Billy Wayne prayed over the corpse and touched its cold brow, and how Lanny blinked his eyes just like Lazarus must have and whispered, "More light." And the bishop answered, yes, Billy Wayne did seem to be on his way to sainthood, but the path, he cautioned, was rugged and tortuous. We felt honored as a community to have nurtured such a special child. (At least those of us not busy insinuating that Billy Wayne was the AntiChrist felt honored.) Two of the older nuns claimed to have witnessed an aura around Billy Wayne, said it was crimson and shimmered like heat on blacktop; Sister Mary Kevin said that ambrosia lingered in his wake.

Still there are some things that you quite simply cannot escape. One is fate, another heredity, though sometimes we wonder if they aren't one and the same. That summer, while at the very pinnacle of his spiritual powers, Billy Wayne took his first step along that aforementioned rugged path and tripped. That summer our novice, regrettably, inevitably, discovered his manhood.

What happened was this. On one of his regular evening visits to the infirm, Billy Wayne had occasion to comfort and aid one Earlene DeBastrop, a poor young thing being treated for female problems. Earlene lived alone with her eighty-year-old Papaw in Bawcomville out by the paper mill.

Billy Wayne tapped on the door, opened it, stuck his head into the room. "May I come in?" he said.

"Sure you can."

Until his eyes adjusted to the crepuscular light, Billy Wayne squinted toward the bed when he spoke.

"You're a tad young for a priest, ain't you, Father?" Earlene said.

"Well, you see, I'm not actually a priest. And call me Billy Wayne."

"If you ain't no priest, why you wearing that sorry black what's-it then?"

"Cassock," he said. "I'm a novitiate."

Earlene wondered how did that explain anything. She told Billy Wayne to take a load of his mind. Then she said he might move his chair closer by her bed. She switched off the gooseneck lamp on her nightstand. "I need to speak with someone."

"That's what I'm here for," Billy Wayne said. "Your name is Earlene?"

"That's right."

"Well, Earlene, I'm listening."

"I need forgiveness."

"Yes."

"You can do it, can't you?"

"You mean Confession?"

"Yes."

"No, I can't do that, Earlene."

"Please."

"I told you I'm not a priest."

"You're somebody. I need to tell somebody. I mean that's what Confession's about, having a somebody there, isn't it? Shit, otherwise we could just pray our sins away. We don't need God's forgiveness at all, Billy Wayne, 'cause that's automatic. Don't you get it? We need a person to tell us we're still good after all we've done."

Billy Wayne pondered what Earlene had said. She made

an unsettling kind of sense to him in a way that he couldn't quite figure just yet.

"Just listen to me," Earlene said, "and when I'm finished, tell me it's all right. Tell me that people will want me still, that I'm not just a cracked pitcher like Papaw says."

Billy Wayne nodded, placed his missal on the nightstand. "I'll close the door," he told Earlene. He stood.

"And shut down the air conditioner at the window," she said. "I want to whisper and I need you to hear."

Earlene, fragrant with lilac water, began. "Bless me, Billy Wayne, for I have sinned."

Billy Wayne shut his eyes, dropped his forehead onto his folded hands, smelled Earlene's womanly substance on the bedsheets, and listened.

"These are my sins," she said. "I did it to this boy, Marzell Swan, and Marzell Swan did it to me. Then Marzell and me went all the way."

Suddenly it was like Billy Wayne was underwater and couldn't breathe, couldn't talk, couldn't fathom this whirlpool in which he was drowning. He could not imagine what "it" could possibly mean that was different from "all the way," and he had only a clinical notion of "all the way," but he understood from the solemn tone of Earlene's voice, from her tears, and from his own light-headedness that it must be miraculous, all of it.

Earlene continued. "Every blessed night for three months no matter where we was, we was on it. Just like frogs in a slough."

Billy Wayne knew about the frogs, all their furious croaking and the other moist noises. He saw them now,

coupled, wet, the jerky little spasms, that frothy business
clinging to their slimy thighs.

"But I couldn't stop myself. I didn't love Marzell. I didn't
even want him around. He's just a dumb redneck shit-
kicker. Excuse my French, Billy Wayne. All's he cared
about was driving his truck and working his little wand
inside me somewhere. But every night I ached for him."

Billy Wayne opened his eyes. He heard a call for Dr.
King on the hospital intercom. He saw himself as if from
the ceiling, a figure in black, sitting on the edge of his
chair, bent toward a bed on which a woman in a white slip
sat, pillows at her back. He wondered what he would
do.

"It's wrong, I know it. You're supposed to love a boy
first," Earlene said.

Billy Wayne wanted to say something. He heard the
whisper of the vinyl seat cushion as he stood.

Earlene looked up at him. "Billy Wayne?" she said.

"It's all right," he said. He lifted a damp curl from her
cheek. "It's all right."

And whatever else they whispered in the dim light of
that semiprivate room so stirred our Billy Wayne that, well,
one thing led to another and so on. In the morning they
were gone.

Monsignor Pargoud lapsed into drink directly upon
learning of Billy Wayne's nuptials some weeks later, and
no one, except perhaps the bishop, blamed him. When the
good Sisters were at last unable to conceal his behavior,
the monsignor was retired to a retreat house in Mount
Lebanon. His room overlooked the exact spot where Clyde
Barrow drove into an ambush in 1934.

As disappointed as we all were with Billy Wayne, we were duly impressed with his ambition. Billy Wayne worked two jobs to support his youthful bride. Mornings, he fried doughnuts at the King Louis XIV Doughnut Stand on Highway 80, and afternoons sprayed roaches for Haddad Pest Control. In less than a year, Billy Wayne managed to take a mortgage out on a shotgun house on the Southside and fix it up with wallpaper and linoleum. And when, after two years of marriage, the couple remained childless, we assumed that Earlene's "female problems" had rendered her barren, and we wished the pair a long and prosperous life together.

However, prosperity, as you may have imagined, was simply not in the cards. Billy Wayne was a Fontana, after all. One Saturday morning Earlene paid an unexpected visit to the King Louis XIV and in front of customers and all alluded to Billy Wayne's ineffectual performance of his husbandly duties. "You can be a husband," she said, "or you can be a priest." Billy Wayne could have made excuses. There were, after all, these two jobs, and the overtime, and the fix-it chores around the cottage that kept him busy until all hours and often left him exhausted come bed time. He could have whispered that to Earlene right there at the counter, held her hand, asked her to please understand. But, in fact, they had had this conversation previously, and she had told him to quit one of the jobs. No, they both understood that there was something else, something unutterable and malevolent between them, though only Billy Wayne knew that the something else was fear.

Whenever he did make love to Earlene, Billy Wayne heard the voice of Monsignor Pargoud explaining how any

further Fontana babies would likely be cloven-hoofed and
tailed, and so isn't it provident that the Lord has called
you to the priesthood, my son. And that made it difficult
for Billy Wayne to keep his mind on the business at hand.
He worried that his selfish and unbridled passion could
result in tragedy for his family. Further, he knew that any-
thing as pleasurable as sex with Earlene, indeed, anything
at all that caused one to abandon reason, if only momen-
tarily, duty or not, was sin itself or the near occasion to it.

Earlene announced that she had needs and womanly
aspirations and fully intended to realize them and so could
no longer shackle herself to six feet of bad luck. She was
filing for divorce, she said, and moving away.

Billy Wayne brushed some powdered sugar from his chin
and said, "Who you been talking to, Earlene?" But Ear-
lene was gone, and here he was an ex-husband-to-be at
twenty-one, devoid of physical love, spiritual vocation, and
emotional companionship. Billy Wayne did not give him-
self time to think, but did the irrational thing and remar-
ried as soon as he could. The bishop, still smarting from
his previous contacts with Billy Wayne perhaps, had refused
to annul the first marriage and so added excommunica-
tion to Billy Wayne's considerable troubles. The hasty
marriage may have been Billy Wayne's way of proving to
himself, if not to Earlene, that he could overcome his fears.

Nine months after the wedding, Tami Lynne delivered
their first child at the new charity hospital. The birth was
uneventful: the boy weighed nearly eight pounds, had ears
flattened to his skull in the Fontana style, screamed heal-
thily enough and all. But hours later, a nurse discovered a
problem. Turns out that the baby was born with a heart

wired like a pinball machine. Tami Lynne phoned Billy Wayne at the doughnut shop and told him to hurry to the hospital. "They found something the matter with the boy, Billy Wayne. I don't know what I'll do."

"Now calm down, sugar. Tell me what's wrong."

"His heart's deranged."

"I'll be there directly."

When he arrived at the ICU, Billy Wayne found his wife in a wheelchair staring at their baby, wrapped in tubes and tape, asleep in a glass case. She was crying. The unit was bright, shadowless, and cold. A nurse talked on a green wall phone. She had a finger in her other ear and was smiling. In an incubator beside Billy Wayne's son was this baby no bigger than a yellow perch.

"My God," Billy Wayne said.

"Maybe it was all that coffee I drank," Tami Lynne said.

Billy Wayne massaged her shoulders. "That's foolish, you hear," he said. "I'll talk to the nurse."

Billy Wayne learned that his son had gone from a jaundiced yellow to blue to white to pink and back again, that a specialist, a Dr. Rangaraj, had arranged for a series of tests to be run that morning, and beyond that, no one knew what the cause of the problem might be.

Billy Wayne watched the monitor attached to his son, saw how the erratic pulse suddenly and inexplicably twitched from a sedate 120 up to 275 and then jumped again to 400 as if a silver ball were jammed on a coil. He knelt on the floor by Tami Lynne. "It's my fault," he said.

"You mean that silly curse they talk about?"

It was not what he had meant at all, but he said yes, the curse. "My family has had problems with this sort of thing before," he said. What really concerned Billy Wayne, however, was not the figurative sins of his fathers, but his own blatant transgressions. Hadn't he turned his back on his sacred vocation, chosen the life of the body over that of the spirit? And does not he that soweth to the flesh reap corruption? Hadn't he also torn asunder what his God had joined together? And will not this God punish such pride? And was this not the trembling wages of his sin before him now, crying in its troubled sleep?

Tami Lynne stroked Billy Wayne's hair. "Look at me, honey," she told him. "Don't you worry none. We'll be all right, the three of us."

"I should have realized." Billy Wayne prayed. He wanted to know the boy, that's all. Just a little while, maybe just hold it, make it smile. That's when the monitor's alarm buzzed and the red light over the unit door flashed. The nurse, who had been on the phone again, hurried over, made sense of the monitor's paperwork, took a hypodermic syringe from her pocket, and inserted the needle into the baby's IV tube. In thirty seconds, the pulse was 150. "He's a tough little guy," she said.

"Nurse, has my boy seen a priest?" Billy Wayne said.

"No. Would you like me to call Father Corkery now?"

There may not be time, he thought. "No thank you. But perhaps you could help me with this."

The nurse held the glass top of the incubator open while Billy Wayne dripped water from an eyedropper on his son's forehead. He said, "I baptize you Duane Pargoud Fontana, in the name of the Father and of the Son and of the Holy Ghost. Amen."

Thus Billy Wayne performed his one and only baptism

on his dying son, but Duane survived. Doctors stabilized the heartbeat with drugs, and although hopeful, advised the parents to plan a prudent life for Duane. So distraught was the new father that he considered a vasectomy and only an article in the *Sons of Mary Newsletter* convinced him otherwise. He did, however, take precautions against another birth, at least until the evening he finally succumbed to the relentless maternal pleadings of Tami Lynne.

A year and a half later, a second child arrived. The unfortunate Moon Pie was born with two tiny cartilaginous appendages resembling flippers more than legs. The doctors could offer no explanation for this cruelly atavistic deformity and seemed genuinely embarrassed in the presence of this demi-child as if they wished not to witness what they had wrought. Billy Wayne took the tragic birth as a further divine repudiation of his life and suffered guilt so overwhelming that he endured a prolonged season of lassitude, losing heart and energy for all matters connubial and financial.

Tami Lynne, who had never rehearsed herself for anything other than domestic duties and wedded bliss, steeled her feminine will, went to work as a checker at Safeway, and found herself a lover. Found him, in fact, back in the meat department.

Besides being the assistant meat manager at Safeway, Russell Sikes was a kind of local celebrity. Russell wrote the horoscope column for the weekly *Twin City Shopper* and even made the national news one time. On the night of July 17, 1979, Russell and his cousin Johnny Ray Lafond were bream fishing on Bayou D'Arbonne when they were abruptly bathed in a sultry, fragrant magenta light, which caused them to swoon, collapse in a heavenly rapture, and altogether surrender their consciousness. They were found the next morning by a mosquito-abatement crew. Russell and Johnny Ray were incoherent and disoriented, wandering along the Louisiana & Missouri tracks down by Elysian Fields. Johnny Ray's hearing aid was gone, but miraculously he could hear clearly every word the police said and realized for the first time that his cousin Russell had a speech impediment. The pair claimed to have been abducted by alien creatures and baptized in the river of cosmic love and understanding.

Now it was Russell Sikes's opinion, one he shared with Tami Lynne over coffee at Morrison's Cafeteria, that the Fontanas just might be from Venus, the morning star, not the city of Italy.

"Those little spacemen sauté your brain, Russell?"

"Look, you don't just all of a sudden show up in history as some full-grown swamp man like they say what's-his-face did."

"Peregrine."

"Not if you were born on earth you don't. People on earth have a past. Think about it."

"I'm thinking you ought to get yourself out of the meat locker once in a while."

"I'm serious," Russell said. He used a napkin to wipe his forehead. "Just like a Capricorn to look at the truth and not see it." He told Tami Lynne that Venusians have been dumping their genetic undesirables on us for two centuries, ever since they discovered a special molecular transport process at about the time the first beaver pelts were being canoed down the Ouachita from Arkansas.

"You're so cute when you're excited, Russell." Tami Lynne smiled. She checked her watch. "It's two-thirty."

"Hitler was a Venusian," Russell said. "So is John McEnroe, the tennis player, not the stock boy in produce."

"We've got us one half hour. Maybe we could drive out to the levee before work, Russell." Tami Lynne ran her tongue along her lips. "If you catch my drift."

Now for all those several years, Billy Wayne remained unaware that his wife and his butcher were carrying on an affair between split shifts at the market. Even the occasional appearance of beef brisket in the freezer failed to arouse his suspicions. Billy Wayne was too occupied with his penance to notice, that penance being a tireless attention to his afflicted sons. He devoted himself entirely to his children now as only a man fueled by guilt truly can. Billy Wayne knew that this selfless regard for their well-being would not alleviate his suffering and understood that if he felt incomplete, well, that was hardly important anymore.

So mornings he baked, fed the boys biscuits and gravy, put the finishing touches on Duane's arithmetic homework, made their beds. Tongues wagged in town. Some joked that the Fontanas finally had themselves a woman— "Billie" Wayne. Evenings, while the boys watched color TV, Billy Wayne got out the ammonia and car wax and shined up Moon Pie's wheel chair. Then he plugged the battery into the charger he'd bought at Sears. When he finished, Billy Wayne went out to the porch to sit with Tami Lynne.

"You be sure to thank Russell Sikes for those cutlets he brought by tonight, Tami Lynne."

"I'll be sure to."

If the wind was off the river and Billy Wayne could smell the paper mill, he'd be reminded of Earlene and he'd go quiet, then say, "Good night, sugar," and retire to their room. Except for the night Tami Lynne spoke up.

"Sit down, Billy Wayne."

Billy Wayne sat. Tami Lynne stood. She leaned back against the banister. "We haven't been, you know, compatible, not since Moon Pie was born. Not so it mattered anyway. That's just not good for a marriage, is it?"

Billy Wayne looked away.

"You're a fine daddy, Billy Wayne; the boys adore you. But you're not just their daddy. You're my husband, too." Tami Lynne knelt on one knee before him. She took his hand, said, "I love you, Billy Wayne Fontana. Look at me. Please." She fixed her eyes on his. "I have my needs. You understand that, Billy Wayne?"

"Of course I do."

"Do you?"

"Understand?"

"Have needs?"

"Lots of them. Some are just stronger than others right now."

"So you do know that our needs sometimes make us less sympathetic than we want to be."

"I know that." Billy Wayne walked to the screen door and stopped. He looked into the house and watched Moon

Pie push himself across the kitchen floor on his skate-board. He turned. Tree frogs hummed in the tupelo.

Tami Lynne said, "What is it, Billy Wayne?"

"Nothing."

"What's the matter then? Am I ugly, Billy Wayne? Tell me."

"It's just that when I have the passion for you, I think about Moon Pie and I . . ."

"You what?"

"Well, when I think it could happen again, I become unmanned."

Tami Lynne, convinced that this was her only chance at domestic harmony, confessed her six years of infidelity with Russell Sikes, said she'd quit her job, naturally enough, pledged her undying love for Billy Wayne, and would make an appointment to have her tubes tied tomorrow. And then at long last, Billy Wayne awoke from his languor, rubbed the penance from his eyes, and got on with his life, confident for the first time in ages. Stirred by the immensity and eloquence of Tami Lynne's gesture of love, he dutifully returned to work as an exterminator and to his obligations as a devoted and satisfying husband. Billy Wayne felt renewed and cleansed as if he had received a sacrament.

All of which brings us back to where we started this story—with the abduction. Except for the one crucial matter: Whenever Tami Lynne barbecued a rack of ribs, say, or browned andouille for her jambalaya, she'd be reminded of Russell Sikes. More and more often she caught herself driving over to the Safeway to have Russell grind her some

of that real lean beef. She'd say, "Why you smiling, Rus-
sell Sikes? Got yourself a girlfriend from space?" Russell
would all the time tell Tami Lynne how he was just wait-
ing for her to come on back to him. It was in the stars,
he'd say. Tami Lynne missed that—the security of know-
ing the future. No, she didn't believe in astrology. She
believed in Russell Sikes. Six months after her aforemen-
tioned disclosure and avowal, Tami Lynne, realizing that
she had tragically underestimated her fascination with
Russell Sikes, but not without some misgiving, told Billy
Wayne that she was leaving him for the butcher.

Nature cannot abide that anyplace should be empty.
Neither, evidently, could Russell Sikes. Two months after
the disappearance from Monroe of Tami Lynne's hus-
band and child, Russell Sikes moved himself, his cleaver,
knives, and sharpening steel, his astrology newsletters, his
oxblood work boots, and his white coats into the Fontana
shotgun. Where nothing had recently been, now slept
Russell Sikes. The new arrangement, however, did not
please the grieving Moon Pie. Perhaps he understood this
new domestic order as an affront to his hope for the
reappearance of his daddy and his bubba, both of whom
he missed so terribly much. Moon Pie sulked and moaned
much of the day. He grew slovenly, would just leave the
dried cat food stuck on the tread of his gray tires. The
plaid blanket that covered his vestigial limbs was so sticky
with spilled root beer and half-sucked candy that Scarlet,
his cat, no longer leaped up on his wheelchair to nuzzle

and purr on her master's lap. Moon Pie was, we feared, eroding, you know, the way a river cuts a bank, slowly to start, but soon—all at once.

Meanwhile, in his column, Russell Sikes predicted that Billy Wayne and Duane would be found by Thanksgiving, alive, healthy, and repentant. He wrote that Billy Wayne would plead guilty to kidnapping and would serve seven years in Angola, but would emerge like a butterfly from a chrysalis—beautiful, cheerful, and ready to taste the sweetness of life. Tami Lynne asked Russell if she should set a place for Duane at Thanksgiving dinner. But the pair were not found. The *Twin City Shopper*, embarrassed, hired a woman from Calhoun to do its horoscope. Russell was baffled and depressed but undeterred. In early December, he placed an anonymous phone call to Sheriff Tidwell, suggesting that the Fontanas were at the bottom of Horseshoe Lake. Only, of course, it was not anonymous on account of Russell's pronounced speech impediment.

After the Police Jury authorized the search, and after nothing human was recovered from Horseshoe Lake, Sheriff Tidwell dropped in on Russell at Tami Lynne's and emphatically suggested that he make no further anonymous calls. "That lisp gives you away, son." Russell asked Buddy to step out on the porch. He didn't want to upset Tami Lynne and the child. Russell watched the front door as he whispered to the sheriff about the dream that had been plaguing him for the past two weeks.

"It's the same thing every night, Sheriff. It's eating at me."

"Do tell," Buddy said. He tipped the Stetson up a bit on his forehead, folded his arms, and listened.

"First there's Duane, only you can't hardly tell it's Duane, you just know it is. He's floating on his back inside a white coffin and he's looking right at you and he's smiling. That's it. Pretty weird, huh?"

"I'd say so."

"Then you see Billy Wayne and he's being suffocated by this damp, black blanket. Then it gets stranger." Russell sneaks another glance at the door, takes Buddy by the elbow, and leads him down the steps to the walk. "There's Moon Pie and he's swimming in this river or pond, you don't know what. He's got these whiskers, kind of like a seal, and he's diving under the wake of a passing houseboat."

Buddy took a breath and put his arm on Russell's shoulders. "I'm not Freud or one of those guys like that," he said, "but it strikes me that just maybe there might be some guilt at work here, Russell."

"Sheriff, you got to believe me; something's going to happen. My dreams don't lie. I'm afraid to sleep anymore."

"I'm going to give you some free advice, son. If you can't sleep nights, get up and watch TV. Just stay off the phone, or else."

Later on, after all the mess, Buddy Tidwell would remark on the curious accuracy of Russell's visions, how the bodies were all discovered kind of like the way he described and so on. Buddy found it all creepy and remarkable and was glad he didn't have to try to explain it to anyone. Of course, by that time, Russell Sikes was no longer in Monroe and so was unable, we imagined, to savor this moment of vindication. But let's not get ahead of our story.

Shortly before Christmas, then, Tami Lynne drove Moon Pie out to the mall to watch Santa Claus parachute in over the parking lot. She hoped a chat with Santa might boost the boy's spirits. Santa wore a camouflage jumpsuit and landed in the bed of a Chevy pickup. Moon Pie told Santa he didn't suppose he'd find his daddy or Duane under the Christmas tree. Santa stole a glance at Tami Lynne and said, "That's right, Junior, so tell Santa what else you all want." Moon Pie pulled a medical catalogue out from the knapsack looped around the handgrip of his chair and showed Santa a deluxe, long-life battery that was guaranteed to keep him motoring for a hundred miles between charges. And that's what he got for Christmas.

Now he no longer had to depend on his mother or on the unreliable Russell Sikes to charge his batteries. Now he was free and independent, he figured, though still only seven years old. He bought bicycle reflectors for his spokes and for the back upholstery. He strapped a flashlight to the armrest with duct tape. Twice, the state troopers found him tooling down the Interstate toward Shreveport—looking for his daddy, he told them. Tami Lynne was decidedly troubled. She indicated to her son that he'd best cease his vexatious behavior pronto or else he'd lose his battery altogether. Of course, both she and Moon Pie recognized an empty threat when they heard one. What all was she supposed to do when she had to work, for one thing? Hire some out-of-work cotton chopper to push the boy home from school or what? So Moon Pie was again everywhere he was not supposed to be, it seemed, whirring along in his supercharged machine. One thing he liked especially was driving through the Zodiac Car Wash while Cecil

Pilcher, the attendant, sprayed him with the pressure hose. Loved to be dripping wet, Moon Pie did. He'd get soaked like that, then motor into Safeway, head for the meat room, and sit there icing up while Russell Sikes sawed through sides of swine.

Tami Lynne stood him up on a kitchen chair and gave him a talking-to. "Honey, you're going to drive me mental if you don't stop these joyrides. Is that what you want? You want your momma in the psychopathic ward over to St. Francis?"

"No, Mam, I don't."

"So why do you do it?"

Moon Pie tapped his flipper on the seat cushion and mumbled he didn't know why.

"Look at your momma. Don't you know I worry about you, baby? You'll get yourself killed one of these days."

Maybe Moon Pie thought, "Who cares anyway with my daddy and brother gone," but he kept quiet.

"I've got an idea. If you're good, keep to the sidewalks and all, stay in the neighborhood, I'll buy you that lizard you've had your eye on at Dr. Doolittle's."

"The chameleon?"

"The greenish guy."

"That's him."

Evidently he wanted that lizard, because he was extra good, even started conversing politely with Russell Sikes. He named the lizard Duane Junior.

It had been nearly a year since the kidnapping and still not a trace of father and son. That's when Saterfiel's Dairy got in on the act and printed a red-and-white photo of Duane on its half-gallon cartons of whole milk and below it a phone number to call should you see the boy. The *Citizen* ran a feature story marking the anniversary and printed a front-page picture of Tami Lynne pouring Saterfiel's milk onto Moon Pie's Sugar Pops, Tami looking wistful-like, Moon Pie crossing his eyes like he does. Seeing her boy's face in the refrigerator every day had a soothing effect on Tami Lynne. It was rather like having her son in the house again. She'd leave the milk carton on the table at meals and sometimes even ask it questions. So when Saterfiel's replaced Duane with LSU's football schedule on their milk cartons, Tami Lynne was devastated. She wanted Duane back desperately, the flesh-and-blood Duane, and his father with him. She now accepted her complicity in the crime that had divided her peculiar little family. Her three men could be unsettling at times, she knew, but they were hers at least, and she belonged with them. She became petulant with Russell Sikes and irritated with his predictions. She simply refused to listen any longer to his dreams.

By the way, Russell was no longer bothered by the Fontana Death Dream. By this time Russell was dreaming of a world in which we were all Arabs. In this world, you all had to pray at certain times. Even if you were on a bass boat, say, on Black Bayou Lake and a storm was blowing, and it was prayer time, why you had to stop and pray. It was good, this Arab world, Russell said. Like all visionaries, he felt the compulsion to share his version of tomorrow with anyone wise and kind enough to listen. Russell printed his gospel on colorful leaflets and tacked them up wherever he could, like at markets and washeterias. At the bottom of each leaflet was his phone number and an invitation for readers to call. But no one did. Ever. Seems not many cotton farmers or field hands were crazy about the notion of their grandchild wearing a burnoose. Russell understood and told Johnny Ray that, after all, you had to expect people to be skeptical at first. Tami Lynne, though, went way beyond skepticism the night they had the big fight at the Sho Bar. The Sho Bar down Louisville by the bridge was their spot, Monday their night. Was hardly a soul in the place when Tami Lynne dropped a quarter in the jukebox and punched up George Jones's "If My Heart Had Windows." They sat at a corner table.

"You say his name's John?" Tami Lynne asked.

"Not his, its. They don't have sexes like we do." They were discussing the chief medical officer of the spaceship that had shanghaied Johnny Ray and Russell. The one who had massaged a hot, redolent, vision-kindling salve onto Russell's brain. "John Alice Stansbury."

Tami Lynne stared into Russell's tiny blue eyes.

"Well, they have a right to names, don't they, sweetheart?" He told her how John Alice was with the crew that had built the pyramids in Cairo, not the Illinois one, and had supervised the Venusian hatchery at Poverty Point.

Tami Lynne fished a Tylenol from her purse and washed it down with a swallow of beer.

"Think about it now. Didn't I tell you they'd find a body on the levee and didn't it happen just like I said?"

"Russell, this is Monroe. They find a couple of bodies a year down by that slough."

"With the ears missing?"

"Can't we ever talk about normal things? Phone bills, vacations, dental appointments?"

"There's something I didn't tell you about that night on the spaceship."

"I don't want to hear this, Russell."

"They're fixing to come back for me shortly."

"You're talking like an imbecile, Russell."

"You can come with me, you and Moon Pie."

"All right, that's it, Russell." Tami Lynne stood. "I'm going for a drive now. And then I'm going home. When I get there I want to find you reading the sports page or polishing the furniture. And I want all of those magazines gone, and the charts and the dreambooks. All of it. If we're going to stay together it will be on this planet."

Moon pie found the note addressed to his momma taped to the fridge. Russell wrote that it was time for him to go, that this part of his life—the butcher part—was clearly finished, that he was going to a town called Sedona, Arizona, because he'd seen it in a dream, and not to worry, he wrote, Duane and his daddy would return the following Wednesday afternoon. Which they did.

Perhaps on that dank and feverish night one hundred and forty-something years ago when Peregrine Fontana mounted his found woman on their rude bed of damp moss and musky pelts, and groaned and ground two lives into being, it became the cruel and unavoidable fate of the Fontanas to endure heroically or mindlessly a century or more of misery and affliction and to be ultimately vanquished by his uncomprising and degenerate gene. Or does the responsibility for tragedy rest not with fate and heredity but with a man and his fatal act of will? Perhaps, in the end, it does not matter. A choice is made, a step taken, a stone loosed, the landslide begun.

The particular avalanche that buried our three Fontanas started precisely at noon on September 7th of this year, four months after Billy Wayne drove up the Winnsboro Road into town, Duane asleep in the bed of the pickup, pulled into his driveway, and walked up to the house holding Duane on his hip. He saw Tami Lynne at the kitchen table and opened the door. Tami Lynne looked up from her crossword puzzle and was struck dumb. She thought she might be having a Russell-like mystical experience. Here was this ventriloquist and his dummy, both dressed in seersucker suits and white bucks, their hair short, parted, and slicked down with pomade like they were about to perform on the *Good Morning, Ark-La-Miss* television program. Now they might be aliens or angels even, but why were they in her kitchen? Indeed, daddy and son looked more like they'd just attended a weekend sales conference at the Holidome and not survived a year in the swamp.

"We got stuck in traffic," Billy Wayne said. Duane muttered something in his sleep. "Accident on Highway 15 in Alto, otherwise we'd have been home some hours ago."

"Billy Wayne?"

"Forgive me, Tami Lynne."

"Oh, my God."

"I am truly sorry for what I have done. I had no right to take the boy. I know that. I was just . . ."

"That's over between Russell and me, Billy Wayne. You

are home where you belong now." She helped him undress Duane. She kissed the boy and slipped him under the sheets in his bed. "I love you again," she told Billy Wayne.

The first thing Billy Wayne did was to hire himself a well-connected Italian lawyer from Natchitoches who happened to be the governor's chief fund-raiser. The first thing that Duane said to Moon Pie was, "I thought you'd be walking by now." Meanwhile, Tami Lynne, grateful beyond simple words, interceded with Buddy Tidwell, who spoke with Judge Noble Osborne, who in turn received a phone call from the governor's office and then met with the D.A. to set a date for the hearing. Moon Pie looked at his big brother, smiled, and said, "You ain't the only Duane here now."

We learned at the hearing that the pair had spent the better part of their exile in an abandoned hunting lodge on Davis Island, living off nutrias and fish mostly, and that was why—the swamp, the spring floods, and all—Billy Wayne did not take Moon Pie along. He told Judge Osborne that he'd done a lot of thinking in a year and a half and realized now that even though his motive may have been honorable—he had only wanted to be with his boy—his method was sinful. In short, he explained, he had recaptured some of his old religious zeal and knew the Lord wanted him to return to Monroe. Duane was all for staying away. At any rate, a deal was fixed. Billy Wayne was ordered to perform community service work for two years. Given Billy Wayne's background and experience,

and perhaps mindful of past debts, Judge Osborne deter-
mined that the work should be done at St. Francis Hospital.

While their parents spent the week in court, Moon Pie
and Duane got reacquainted. Moon Pie introduced his
brother to Duane Junior, and the former was charmed with
his namesake, the way its eyes moved independently, the
way it changed color like a river at dawn, the way it puffed
up that deal under its chin while sitting on his shoulder.
Duane explained to Moon Pie how he and his daddy would
trap nutria, how they tasted like chicken. Moon Pie told
Duane about Russell Sikes and his knives and leaflets, but
not about the dreams he'd overheard him tell the sheriff.
About the bobbed tail on the lizard, Moon Pie explained
as to how his friend in second grade, Bobby Joe Wilcoxen,
told him lizards would grow a new tail if you cut theirs off.
Turns out it was some kind of salamander he meant.

Billy Wayne reckoned it was more like browsing through
a museum of his childhood than properly being at home
again. After all, so much had changed at St. Francis. Where
the grape arbor had been sat the attendant's shack for the
new parking lot. The ornate chapel with its marble altar
and stained-glass windows was now the ontology lab;
another chapel, in the unadorned contemporary style,
occupied a corner of the new pediatric wing just about
where the tamale shack and Soul City Records had once
stood.

Before punching in that first Monday morning back to
work, Billy Wayne sat at a Formica table in the cafeteria
and smelled the reassuring and familiar cigarette smoke
and frying meat, aromas that drew him back to childhood

meals in this very room. He peppered his poached eggs, sugared his coffee, opened the morning paper, and read the headlines. He once would sit just here, in the window light facing the cafeteria line, with Sister Helen. She came from Ireland and would tell him stories about her da's potato farm and would answer his questions about the world beyond the hospital walls. Billy Wayne recalled her telling him, "People like us with the vocation do not marry, that's all. We haven't the time. There's prayer and there's work; the indisposed ones are more important than the self. Remember that, Billy Wayne." Sister Helen, he'd learned, was back in Cork now. In fact, there were very few nuns left, none of whom he had known. In their places was an army of efficient, vigorous, self-assured technicians. Medicine had become a business, not a vocation. That's what he thought, we think.

He took his notebook and a pen from his shirt pocket and wrote this: "I have the sense of starting over, as if the fourteen years had not passed, as if I could save both the world and my soul." And then he scribbled over some lines and began a second page: "I fear that nothing will work out." And then this was circled in the middle of the page: "What God has joined together." And below that, underlined: "It's summer, 1972." The notebook was found later on by Sheriff Tidwell on the front seat of Billy Wayne's pickup.

Billy Wayne folded the paper to the classifieds. Under the personals, he found Earlene's Insurance and wrote down the phone number. He took a last sip of his coffee, carried his tray to the conveyor belt, and walked to Maintenance to start his new job.

Billy Wayne's job was to scrub, disinfect, and otherwise prepare vacated rooms for incoming patients. He remembered being in these rooms years ago, sitting at the bedside, spooning custard into a toothless mouth or praying at night with a cancered woman scheduled for surgery. He felt a profound sense of loss, a loss of self, that he couldn't explain. His sadness at work began to affect his homelife. It's not that he was mean or uncaring, simply withdrawn. Nights he'd sit in the rocker on the porch, stare at the banister, and once in a while shake his head a bit. Do that until the last light went off in the house, then go to bed.

Tami Lynne startled him. "I brought you out a Dr Pepper, Billy Wayne."

"Thank you."

"I sure hope this is a phase you're going through."

"What's that?"

"Not speaking with any of us," she said. Tami Lynne kissed the top of his head and rested her cheek there. "I know it must be hard, getting used to the world again."

"A bit."

"What is it you're thinking about all the time?" Tami Lynne sat herself on Billy Wayne's lap. "Maybe if you talked about it."

Billy Wayne looked at her, figured all right, it's been a long time coming, and set out to tell her everything. "How I came to be a kidnapper," he began, "a divorcé, the father of two boys with faulty parts, a derelict husband who drove his wife into the arms of the neighborhood psychic."

"Stop it, Billy Wayne."

"I started out just wanting to do good, be kind to people, that's all, and look what happened."

"It's that hospital. I knew it. Reminding you every day of the little saint you wanted to be. Maybe you just should have gone to prison awhile and worked off some of that guilt." Tami Lynne got up and said, "You're no saint, Billy Wayne. You're just like the rest of us."

"I want to salvage something from my life before it's too late."

"You son of a bitch, Billy Wayne. What the hell do you call this family you got? We ain't salvage enough for you? Is that it?"

"If you don't want to hear what I have to say, why did you bring it up?"

"You had best come around, Billy Wayne, before you lose it all." Tami Lynne walked to the screen door, opened it, said, "Hear me?" and went on in.

So Billy Wayne never did tell her everything. Like how he knew this misery was his doing, was his punishment sort of, for having repudiated his priestly vocation. For that and for the unsanctified second marriage. Tami Lynne might be the natural mother of his children, he granted that, but Earlene remained his canonical wife, no getting around it.

Meanwhile, Moon Pie wondered what was this hell-hound on his daddy's trail. Here was his daddy home at last, reconciled with wife and sheriff, in the bosom of his family, but for all it was worth, he might as well be gone. It truly was worse for Moon Pie having his daddy at home and still not feeling what it was he could hardly remember ever feeling anymore. He blamed himself. According to Duane, the feral life on Davis Island had been like heaven for him and his daddy. Moon Pie figured that had he been born normal like Duane, they, all three of them, would be on that island now pioneering like the Fontanas of old, the ones he'd heard about at his daddy's knee. He wished he were likable. People liked Duane. Lizards liked Duane. He wished his ears weren't so tiny and flat; he wished he could run, wished he could disappear into a swamp the way Duane could. He wished his brother had carried him on his shoulder instead of that lizard. So he didn't care when Duane leashed the lizard to a fire-ant mound. He just wondered was his brother witless enough to think Duane Junior would eat all those ants before they covered him like a shroud.

The moment Billy Wayne both feared and desired had arrived. The room was as dark as a confessional, as quiet as a sanctuary, and fragrant of the lilac blossoms in the glass vase on the nightstand. He felt a shiver at the back of his neck and switched on the light. He opened the windows, cleared the flowers and get-well cards from the bedside table, and began to swab the floor. But it was too late to scrub away the memory of Earlene deBastrop, the woman for whom he had sacrificed so much—his youth, his future, even his God for a time. And what was it, he wondered, that had driven him into her arms, that had persuaded him to put his world at risk? Billy Wayne closed the door at 412N and sat in perhaps the very chair in which he had heard Earlene's sins so long ago. It was love, he realized, pure and simple, that had done it. And now he knew what he must do.

When Earlene left Billy Wayne, she moved away, but not far away, just across the river in West Monroe. She bought herself a double-wide in a little trailer village near

Kiroli Park and set up, as you know, an insurance busi-
ness right out of her paneled parlor. Earlene had this boy-
friend for seven years, a car salesman at Levon's Cartown,
who threw a lot of business her way, but when he still
hemmed and hawed about divorcing his wife, Earlene
called off the affair. When business was slack, she wrote
country-and-Western songs and sent them off to Tom T.
Hall.

Tami Lynne knew nothing about 412N but could see
that Billy Wayne was driving her away and hurting his
children terribly and told him why don't you stop. Even as
he held Tami Lynne and promised to show more affec-
tion, more consideration, and even though this is precisely
what he wanted to do, to be good, kind, he knew he could
not. He saw the boys now as the fruit of his corruption and
Tami Lynne as an obstacle to his inevitable return to Ear-
lene, a return he believed was divinely ordained even
though he had not spoken to Earlene since that fateful
morning at the King Louis XIV.

This is what happened on September 7th near as we can
tell from what Tami Lynne recalled and what Sheriff Buddy
Tidwell and others surmised. Billy Wayne, who hadn't slept
well that night, who had, in fact, already fed the cat, gone
to the 7-Eleven for the paper, done the crossword except
for 65 across and 71 down, and shined his shoes, kissed
Tami Lynne on the forehead and left for work at six-twenty.
Tami Lynne, for her part, was so touched by her hus-
band's unexpected gesture that she lay in bed imagining

kiss after luxurious kiss and determined to do something sweet for Billy Wayne today as he had done for her.

Duane's project for this morning was to build a possum trap out of parts he could salvage from neighborhood dumpsters. Moon Pie could watch, he said, but that's all. So at about nine-thirty, Duane sat reinforcing an orange crate by weaving wire coat hangers through the wooden slats while at the hospital his daddy sat in the cafeteria on his break. Billy Wayne drank iced tea and stared at the phone number he had jotted down on the notebook paper. Billy Wayne walked as far as the pay phone in the lobby before he hesitated, wadded the paper in his palm, and dropped it onto the gray sand of the ashtray.

Tami Lynne heard the boys bickering out back, went to the window, and yelled for them to hush up and be sweet to each other. Moon Pie was crying and said that Duane had tried to haul the battery off his wheelchair. Seems Duane wanted to somehow electrify his possum trap.

"What, you ignorant, Duane?"

"No, Mam."

As soon as Tami Lynne drove off to the fish market in West Monroe, Moon Pie turned on the lawn sprinkler and drove his wheelchair back and forth through the spray. While Moon Pie played car wash, Duane pondered his possum trap. All right then, he figured, he'd use gravity, not electricity. One little wooden whatchamacallit fixed into the frame, he reckoned, would hold the door up, but just barely, so's any vibration would drop the door shut like a guillotine. He fetched his daddy's old electric hand drill out of the shed and ran the extension across the lawn and in through the kitchen window. Damp feet, metal motor housing. You can see it coming, can't you? As soon as Duane squeezed the trigger, he got himself straightened up with 120 volts of electricity, and when an upper filling touched a lower filling in his mouth, he screamed, collapsed on his back, and then his eyes started jiggling in their sockets. Had Tami Lynne returned then as she had intended, she might have found Duane groaning in the dirt, seen how mightily he perspired, and heard how he told Moon Pie how his heart had skipped some beats. She might have brought Duane to the hospital. But Tami Lynne, because of what she heard, did not come directly home.

Billy Wayne had been unable to concentrate on his work all morning. Sure, he'd discarded the phone number; he'd memorized it anyway, and why did he need the number when he knew the address, had even driven by the home twice in the past week and parked a block away and watched until the parlor light came on at dawn and a face peeked out the window? He knew he belonged to Earlene and she to him, else why ever would they have met, married, and pledged undying love? Surely, there had to have been a purpose, reasoned Billy Wayne, elsewise this world and everything in it were all merely accidental and random— not the kind of world a God would create. So when the lunch buzzer sounded in the janitors' room, Billy Wayne decided to forgo the corn dog special in the cafeteria. He took his fate into his hands and drove to Earlene's.

Tami Lynne wanted this to be a special night for her and Billy Wayne to mark the beginning of their new life together, the new life that had begun that morning with a kiss. She planned to make Billy Wayne's favorite that night—crawfish étouffé. She was right to have been patient with him. After all, she had turned away from him once, and that had ended disastrously. So, on leaving the fish market, Tami Lynne drove to Green Acres, this florist shop on Cypress Avenue run by the Oglesbees. Azzie Lee was working the store for her momma, it being a Saturday morning and all. Tami Lynne ordered a half-dozen blood-red roses, and Miss Azzie Lee remarked as to how it must be Tami Lynne's anniversary.

"Why you say that, Miss Oglesbee?"

"Promise you won't tell."

"Tell what?"

"Billy Wayne. He was in here not three minutes ago buying you a dozen of these long-stemmed beauties."

"You must be mistaken."

"No, ma'am, it was Billy Wayne for sure. First time we'd seen each other since . . . well, you know."

"But he's at work."

"And now you both got roses. Won't he be surprised?"

"Just three minutes ago?"

"Yes, ma'am. Drove off down Cypress toward Kiroli Park."

Tami Lynne borrowed Azzie Lee's phone book a minute and looked up under "Insurance" in the Yellow Pages.

"Thank you, Miss Oglesbee."

Moon Pie persuaded Duane he should take a bath on account of he was covered with dirt, and he promised not to tell anyone what had happened. Billy Wayne convinced Earlene to let him speak to her just a moment in the privacy of her office. Duane locked the bathroom door to secure his privacy against his mother's imminent return.

Earlene backed away from Billy Wayne, and without say-
ing a word, drew the blinds shut and locked the front door.
"In the eyes of the Church, Earlene, we're still married.
Always will be." Billy Wayne handed her the roses that he
held out like a torch. It's this other marriage, he went on,
that's the sin, that's damning him to hell. And whatever
else Billy Wayne confessed to her in the dim light of the
mobile home beneath the sofa-sized painting of waves
crashing on a stormy beach so stirred Earlene that, well,
they didn't hear the doorbell ring.

Over the hum of his wheelchair, Moon Pie thought he
heard a thrashing from the bathroom. He called to Duane,
heard the thrashing again and then the racket of metal
and something else hitting against the porcelain. Moon
Pie repeatedly rammed the bathroom door with his chair
to no avail, then went for Russell Sikes's cleaver. Crying
and yelling for Duane to hang on, Moon Pie hacked a
hole through the door panel large enough for him to see
Duane face up in the water, his eyes staring back at the
door. When he had fallen, he had ripped down the vinyl
shower curtain and now lay covered in pastel flowers. His
lips were blue. A trace of blood leaked from his ear. His
heart had shorted out and fluttered to a stop.

What happened after that happened rather quickly. Tami
Lynne found the side door unlocked and walked in. She
discovered the couplers on their backs in the middle of the
living-room floor, their shirts and shoes on, their eyes
closed. She picked up a pen-and-letter holder shaped like
a cat from Earlene's desk. She dropped it and drew their
attention. Earlene reached for her slacks and draped them
over her middle. Billy Wayne sat up.

"How tender," Tami Lynne said. "Father Fontana and his child bride reunited at last."

"Tami Lynne," Billy Wayne said. "What the hell!"

Earlene shook her head. "Jesus Christ, Billy Wayne, you're still trouble."

"More than you know, sweetie," Tami Lynne told her. "Billy Wayne, don't you even think about coming home. The boys and I are done with you."

"Look, I'm sorry," Earlene said.

"Not so sorry as you will be."

"I had no choice, Tami Lynne," Billy Wayne started to explain.

"Yes, I know. This is your salvation."

While Tami Lynne confronted Earlene and Billy Wayne with their tawdry behavior and told her husband that she was leaving him for the second and final time, Moon Pie was driving his machine down DeSiard past Hub Cap City, past the Confederate cemetery, past Cloyd's Beauty School, past the At Your Service Cab Company, all the way to the river. When Tami Lynne found Duane the way he was, naturally she snapped some. Neighbors saw her dragging Duane's naked body across the front lawn and called the police. Tami Lynne was sedated and hospitalized. When the social worker showed up to fetch Moon Pie, he was, as we've said, long gone. He had reached the Forsythe Avenue Boat Dock by then and sat staring past the Twin City Queen into the silty Ouachita. He wished his daddy had never come home. He wished it were like it used to be before Russell Sikes, before the lizard, before the milk cartons. He wished he could disappear like Duane. And then he started the long slide down the hundred-foot boat

ramp. According to the jogger on the levee who witnessed
the whole spectacle, when the chair hit the black water,
Moon Pie was thrown ahead ten feet, went under, sur-
faced, just his head above water. He looked around, smiled,
and then dove. Damnedest thing I ever saw, the jogger
said.

Later that night, Sheriff Tidwell came for Billy Wayne
at Earlene's, asked him to step outside a minute, and con-
fronted him with the news of his two dead boys and a wife
shattered with grief. "And here you are having yourself a
tomcat time of it."

"Oh my God." Billy Wayne slumped to the ground and
kept on moaning and saying, "What have I done? What
have I done?" over and over again. The sheriff let him go
for a bit and then hauled him up by the armpits, sat him
in the back of the cruiser, slapped his face, and shook him
silent.

"Look here, Billy Wayne. I don't know what the hell
you done. I just know you done something. You're the
goddamnedest Fontana of all, you are. No matter how bad
things got out there in the Bottom, the Fontanas always
took care of their children. What went foul with you, Billy
Wayne?"

Billy Wayne cried into his hands.

"This whole parish is finished with you. You best go
somewhere, boy."

Billy Wayne decided to punish himself since we could
not and went back to Chauvin Bottom, where he fash-
ioned himself a crown of nettle as some kind of penance.
The nettle, of course, itched, stung, blotted his skin no
doubt, and within hours swelled his eyes shut. So there he

was, the final Fontana, stumbling through his ancestral home, blind as his daddy, trying to exorcise his demons or atone for this original sin he carried in his genes, when he fell into a nest of cottonmouths. We found him in the morning, bloated with swamp water and venom, and covered with snakes.

Three months have passed since that morning and we have had plenty to think about. At the college, a coed was strangled and stuffed into a dumpster; the parish suffered its worst cotton harvest in twenty-three years; the mill's on strike; two pistoleros shot and killed a 7-Eleven clerk and got away with seventeen dollars; and they're finding tumorous bass in the bayou.

Through it all, the name Fontana has remained on our lips, primarily because of some news—disheartening news, some would say. Earlene deBastrop Fontana is pregnant with Billy Wayne's love child, and that bothers people worse than mayhem and decay. Yesterday, the *Citizen* published an ultrasound photo of the child that was released by the St. Francis PR staff. The caption noted how at that age all fetuses look alike—gills, tails, and all of that—and how you couldn't tell a frog from a child at this point. What you see in the picture is this cranium and the spinal cord. Looks like a number 9 or a banjo.